Laurence Ginnell

The Doubtful Grant of Ireland by Pope Adrian IV. to King Henry II.

Laurence Ginnell

The Doubtful Grant of Ireland by Pope Adrian IV. to King Henry II.

ISBN/EAN: 9783744670746

Printed in Europe, USA, Canada, Australia, Japan

Cover: Foto ©ninafisch / pixelio.de

More available books at **www.hansebooks.com**

THE DOUBTFUL GRANT

OF

IRELAND

BY POPE ADRIAN IV. TO KING HENRY II.

INVESTIGATED

BY

LAURENCE GINNELL

OF THE MIDDLE TEMPLE, BARRISTER-AT-LAW
AUTHOR OF "THE BREHON LAWS," ETC.

Reprinted, with slight revision and re-arrangement, from the
"NEW IRELAND REVIEW"

Dublin
FALLON & CO.
29 LOWER SACKVILLE STREET

1899

PRINTED BY
SEALY, BRYERS AND WALKER,
MIDDLE ABBEY ST.,
DUBLIN.

TABLE OF CONTENTS.

CHAPTER		PAGE
I.	A GENERAL VIEW OF THE GROUND, WITH TEXT OF THE DOCUMENTS TO BE EXAMINED	1
II.	JOHN OF SALISBURY, AND THE EVIDENCE ATTRIBUTED TO HIM	21
III.	CHARACTER OF GIRALDUS CAMBRENSIS	49
IV.	WORKS OF GIRALDUS CAMBRENSIS	71
V.	FURTHER DISCUSSION OF THE PRINCIPAL INSTRUMENT	101
VI.	THE OTHER INSTRUMENTS CONSIDERED, ALL FOUND TO BE SPURIOUS	130
	INDEX	159

THE DOUBTFUL GRANT

OF

IRELAND.

CHAPTER I.

A General View of the Ground, with Text of the Documents to be Examined.

THE charge frequently made that we do not take such interest in our country's history as we ought to do is too true. But it is not universally true. Certain incidents of that history have an irresistible attraction for us. If we except sacred subjects, there is probably no other instance in which the rank and file of a race take to-day such a lively interest in letters written in the twelfth century as the Irish race all over the world take in the documents we are about to consider.

A Bull is a Papal letter, taking its name from the *bubble*-shaped leaden seal which it bears. The letters here in question are five in number, written in the twelfth century, and relating to Ireland. They were probably never sealed with any seal, and are, therefore, not correctly called Bulls, even if genuine; but that name has become so well known in connection with them that the use of it cannot be misunderstood. In the twelfth century they were called *privilegia* or privileges.

According to the strict rules of evidence, documents are

inadmissible until their authenticity is first established. The question of the authenticity of these letters is properly one for historical investigation rather than for argument. Research has so far failed to find their originals, or conclusive proof that originals legitimate and authentic ever existed. But a *prima facie* case for their authenticity having been otherwise made out, and being corroborated by their close resemblance to genuine Papal letters, while at the same time there is in them sufficient divergence from the unquestioned article to excite suspicion, and in the circumstances sufficient to support that suspicion, the question of their authenticity becomes a subject for discussion.

Light has to be sought from the alleged copies of the alleged instruments, from the bearers of those alleged copies and their contemporaries, from the characters of all the persons concerned, and from the general circumstances of the period. A field of considerable scope is thus opened up, and the facts and inferences gleaned therefrom vary with the taste and skill of the gleaners. There may be some who form their opinions first, and investigate afterwards. But when the facts are as well known as they can now be, and conscientiously examined, there is enough in them to occasion the greatest uncertainty; so that one may well be found on either side of this controversy without becoming obnoxious to the charge of mere wilful perversity. And although the result of historical research within the present century has somewhat contracted the scope of the controversy by rendering some of the old positions occupied on both sides no longer tenable, the same research seems to have counterbalanced this by furnishing both sides with new and effective arguments. Some of the evidence on both sides will, at first sight, appear frail, feeble, and scarcely relevant. But if it were gross, palpable and conclusive either way there would no longer be room for argument.

On slight evidence and fine distinctions some of the most important political and business transactions in the world are carried on; on these the fate of a nation occasionally depends; even the most sacred truths of religion, with all they have effected in this world, and all that depends on them in the next, hang by a very slender thread, as does human life itself. We must not disdain or break the filmy threads, but carefully endeavour to disentangle them. Nor must we expect Englishmen, however impartial, to investigate and settle for us this question, affecting as it does the relations between the two countries. We shall notice an occasion on which they evaded that task in circumstances in which they could not have shirked it without risk of reputation had the letters related to England.

In Ireland we find the authenticity of the letters recognised in the seventeenth century by James Ussher, Protestant Archbishop of Armagh; Peter Lombard, Catholic Archbishop of Armagh; and David Rothe, Bishop of Ossory; and in the present century by the ecclesiastical historian, Dr. Lanigan, the Editor of the *Macariæ Excidium*, the Editor of *Cambrensis Eversus*, and the Very Rev. Sylvester Malone, D.D., Vicar-General of Killaloe, writing in the *Dublin Review* for April, 1884, and in the *Irish Ecclesiastical Record* for October, 1891. This latter gentleman, now the ablest and most strenuous upholder of all the letters in question, has written more recently on the same side, but has been obliged to abandon most of his earlier positions without securing any new position. Against their authenticity, we must notice the entire absence of written Gaelic recognition; their repudiation in the seventeenth century by Stephen White, S.J., and by the author of *Cambrensis Eversus;* their repudiation in the present century by Cardinal Moran in the *Irish Ecclesiastical Record* for November, 1872, and by Rev. W. B. Morris in his book, *Ireland and St. Patrick*. The learning and respectability of all the foregoing authorities are admitted.

Many others have written on either side of the controversy, but apparently without having gone to the sources for information, since they make statements either without references or with references which lead to nothing relevant, and even give some references which, when tested, are found to be incorrect. The primary object of some of them at least being not the elucidation of what is admittedly obscure, but the furtherance of current religious or political controversy, they adopt a particular view at the outset. This they are determined not to relinquish. By a process of rejecting rigid facts, twisting pliable ones, and inventing some padding material, they make that preconceived opinion their final conclusion and obtrude it on the public, misrepresenting the purport of the documents and even tampering with their text. They then call for the peremptory closure of the controversy. Such controversy, being wrong in purpose and in method, can have no effect except a bad one. The question at issue, though small, is not to be solved by prejudice or predilection, but by diligent investigation of facts and rational deduction therefrom. Legitimately treated, it is of no practical importance whatever, does not involve either the religion or the politics of our day, and can be properly discussed only by keeping quite aloof from these. The question is purely historical.

Agreement as to the facts among the class of people just mentioned does not secure or connote agreement as to the inferences. For instance, persons who agree that the letters are authentic are most sharply divided as to their significance. Some invoke them with the special object of bespattering Popes and exposing their venality, corruption, and ingratitude towards mankind in general, and towards faithful Ireland in particular; while others draw from them proofs that no Pope ever erred even in political matters, and that Ireland has always been the object of the Pope's special paternal care. These two unhistorical and essentially antagonistic aspirations, originating at the opposite poles of mistaken piety, may safely be left to confute each other. By no possibility can both be true.

From another quarter it has been urged that although neither religion nor morality is involved in the question, nor the doctrine of the Pope's infallibility, still to assume the authenticity of these letters would be tantamount to assuming that the Pope made a shockingly bad choice of an instrument for reducing Ireland to law and order, seeing what the character of Henry II. was, and seeing that the English in the seven hundred years that have elapsed since that time have failed to accomplish the task assigned them. This objection is at best feeble. Of course the consequence suggested, even if it were to follow, should not deter us from endeavouring to find out what is the truth of the matter. But how that consequence is obviated none know better than we who know so well that the object of the English in Ireland has not been the Pope's object, but usually one diametrically opposite. In any case it is far better frankly to withdraw such an objection as this and allow the inquiry to proceed, since it can be so easily confronted and neutralized by examples *in pari materia*. These letters, supposing them to be genuine, would not have constituted a greater Papal mistake than was the conferring of the title of Defender of the Faith upon Henry VIII. of England. Here is an authentic case of the Pope's choosing a singularly unworthy instrument for a purpose at least as intimately connected with his office as was the subject-matter of these letters. And the subsequent use of this title by English Sovereigns shows, too, how willing they are to cling to any honour or advantage derived from the Catholic Church, even when they have ceased to belong to it, and sworn to defend the Protestant. Their conduct in this respect is prevented from being ridiculous only by being royal.

The more closely one studies the two Popes whose letters are in question the more firmly is he convinced that, whether they wrote these letters or not, they resembled most Popes before and since in desiring to promote what they considered the best interests of the Irish people. But like all men dealing with a country with whose circumstances they are not personally acquainted, Popes have had to take their information second-hand, third-hand, or fourth-hand; and the intermediaries have not always been above suspicion. In these circumstances it has been just as easy for the Pope as for anybody else to err in accepting for truth the inventions or the coloured and distorted facts presented to him under the highest guarantee of veracity. Opinions formed on this basis regarding the condition of a country and the best means of improving it, would probably be such as the fictions were specially designed to generate and foster.

The letter to which most effect has always been attributed is that under Pope Adrian's name. In Nicholas Breakspeare we find an excellent illustration of the exaltation of the meritorious humble, and of the democratic constitution of the Catholic Church. A man of the humblest birth, he was, in December, 1154, in recognition of his real personal worth, made Pope, under the name of Adrian IV., and was the only Englishman who ever sat in the chair of St. Peter. The Very Rev. Dr. Malone says:—"There does not appear to be in the domain of history a better authenticated fact than the privilege of Adrian IV. to Henry II." At all events from it the sovereigns of England from Henry II. down to Henry VIII. derived the title of Lord of Ireland which was the only title they used with reference to Ireland. Henry VIII. was the first English king who styled himself King of Ireland. The conclusions arrived at by the best authorities, with regard to the date at which this letter became known in Ireland, show how little warrant there is for the use made of it by partizans.

One writes about the Pope having handed Ireland over to King Henry II., and is quite sure that this letter was Henry's most potent weapon in the conquest of Ireland: another, whose object is different, is not clear about either the facts or the conclusions, but thinks the letter was known in Ireland in 1172, or even earlier. Now, for neither of these positions is there a shadow of historical warrant. On the question of date, most of those who deny the authenticity of the letters believe that they were first made known about 1180, while Rev. Dr. Kelly, a warm supporter of them all, says with regard to Adrian's: "There is not any, even the slightest, authority for asserting that it was known in Ireland before that date (1172), nor for three years later."—*Cambrensis Eversus*, vol. ii., page 440. And the only authority for holding that it was made known in Ireland so early as 1175 is that of Giraldus Cambrensis, which we propose to examine later on. We may then take 1175 as the earliest date at which any but a blind partizan has fixed the first reading of any of these letters in Ireland. Hence, whatever effect they may have had subsequently, they cannot have influenced the Irish in 1172, being then unknown: and for the same reason they cannot have contributed in the slightest degree to Henry's conquest of Ireland.

These letters might, however, have involved, in the twelfth century, matters of discipline and obedience; and a due examination of them demands some knowledge of the faith, the Church discipline, the relations between Church and State, and the general condition of Europe in the twelfth century, and the international politics of that time. According to the conception of human life then current on the Continent, there were scarcely more than two careers worthy of gentlemen—learning and the sword. Learning being available only in and through the Church, men who sought it, with whatever object, were attracted to her; and there being then as now plenty of men with brains far in excess of their piety, the Church sometimes found herself possessed of members, and even of ministers, who seem to us strangely out of place. In addition to what we now consider the normal percentage of young men entering the Church in obedience to vocation or other worthy motive, another and widely different class joined the ranks of the clergy. Cousins of the King, younger sons of the nobility, and other persons conscious of talent or ambition or both, entered the Church deliberately as the surest road for preferment, whether ecclesiastical or civil, without any intention of engaging in missionary or parochial drudgery, but with the fixed purpose of belonging from the outset to the Higher Clergy, who had access to the King's Court. While some of these men remained courtiers all their lives, idle or ill-employed, others, as a natural consequence of their superior culture, from ministers of God, became ministers of the State, lawyers, judges, politicians, secretaries, diplomatists, statesmen, and even soldiers, and the highest civil secular offices were usually filled by them. Royal favourites and connections, frequently mere striplings in their teens, perhaps not in Orders at all, perhaps favoured with Minor Orders *ad hoc*, were appointed to nominal ecclesiastical offices to which the largest revenues were attached, but of which humble and unknown men discharged the real duties. The rich offices were honorary in the inverted sense that their occupants drew the salaries but neglected the duties. In such circumstances, occasional scandals and the presence of odd characters in the sanctuary were phenomena to be expected, and it must in justice be said that they were by no means as numerous as might have been expected. The men of those days were neither all bad nor any of them wholly bad. And as regards those who were really in Holy Orders, it would be easy to name some who, although promoted to high positions in the Church for manifest political reasons, became exemplary occupants of the offices to which they were so raised, effected disciplinary and other improvements which men more holy if less energetic would have found it impossible to effect, became able and zealous churchmen, and sadly disappointed those who had expected to find them pliant tools.

It was a strange and contradictory age, moved by two strong currents; by one towards a higher civilization, by the other back towards barbarism; and sons of the same father are known to have been impelled in those different directions. Some were warmed by the fervour of piety, others by the fervour of wickedness; some by the love of military renown, others by the love of lucre or worse. It was an age of efflorescent Christian chivalry, as exemplified in the Crusades, of general religious unity among Christians, and yet an age of antipopes and local scandals; an age when almost every country in Europe produced, in the same generation, its highest specimen of human perfection and its lowest of human depravity. But, when reading of past ages we are prone to expect something which we do not find in our own, namely, a general uniformity of human character, a thing that never has existed, and certainly does not now exist. It is just possible that from amongst ourselves of the nineteenth century we could match both the best and the worst of the twelfth. For, as if to maintain equilibrium with variety, the great vices of some always draw forth the great virtues of others. As every season has its fashion, so every age has its characteristic moving spirit. That which most filled and moved men's minds in the twelfth century seems to have been an unbounded and insatiable ambition. Of all passions this is the most calculated to excite and disturb high and low, to produce and precipitate complications and changes which affect everybody, to generate in men qualities which in calmer times would have lain dormant, and to bring above the surface some who in calmer times would have remained in lifelong obscurity.

The political condition of most of the nations of Europe was still one of unrest after the convulsions attending and following the disruption of the Western Empire, and their general attachment to the Church, of which the Pope was the first minister, made them look to him as the prime guardian of the Christian fold, and the first enemy of all manner of wrongs and abuses amongst all the nations that accepted the Christian name. They appealed to him for comfort and guidance in all sorts of difficulties, public and private, religious, political, and mixed. Peoples appealed to him against rulers and rulers against one another. All this gave rise to relations between the Pope and States far more numerous and complicated than what are now ordinarily known as the relations between Church and State. Although political action now rarely becomes the duty of the Pope as such, the political condition of a country may occasionally be a matter of great concern to him. This was precisely the condition of the whole of Europe in the twelfth century. The Church was the highest, if not the only, expression of civilization. The Pope's representatives, wherever they went, were bearers of a higher learning and a higher law, as well as of the Gospel. The law they bore was Roman, tempered by Canon Law, which was recognized (however reluctantly) in most of the countries of Europe. In virtue, partly of this law, partly of the condition of things just outlined, and partly of an alleged donation of Constantine the Great, the Pope became a political and international arbiter and umpire at the head of the European States, which, in so far as they were united through him, formed a sort of loose confederation. For him they felt or affected respect, to him they paid deference; and, in spite of the occasional schisms and disorders alluded to, the Pope was powerful with a subtle power, which all recognised, and against which tyrants often chafed. Some of the decretals in the Canon Law seem open to the construction that two or three of the Popes went even beyond this spiritual and moral jurisdiction, and claimed a temporal suzerainty over Europe if not over the entire world. But the acknowledged ambition of all Popes was, as it still is, the apostolic ambition to extend the Church so widely as to include all men, and, consequentially, to bring all men to recognise and submit to the Pope's universal primacy. And even in the cases of Gregory VII. (Hildebrand) and Urban II., who are believed to have extended the temporal power of the papacy to the utmost limits it has ever reached, neither one nor the other of them claimed universal temporal sovereignty. The largest claims they made are fully accounted for by local and temporary causes. The Pope's international position will be found defined in Gosselin's *Pouvoir du Pape au Moyen Age*. Of the hero of Canossa, one of the most learned authorities on events in the Middle Ages says:—" C'est une exagération que d'attribuer à Gregoire VII. des rêves de monarchie et de domination universelles; ce qui le préoccupe, c'est d'affirmer le caractère absolument *catholique* de l'Eglise, et d'assurer la situation *international* de la papauté."—Lucius Lector, *Le Conclave*, page 69.

In these circumstances a considerable amount of business must have been transacted between the Pope and a Catholic prince like Henry II., whose dominions extended from the Cheviot Hills to the Pyrenees. The Pope's power being invoked in all quarters, and being such that it could not be successfully resisted by open force, was frequently met or eluded by fraud. There was a brisk demand for Papal letters and charters, sometimes for strange purposes. To meet this demand, clever ambitious men could scarcely be expected to wait for genuine documents from Rome, especially if those required were such as the Pope was not likely to grant. Consequently, some documents of those times, still existing, are said to be manifest forgeries, and are preserved not for the confirmation of facts, but

as antique specimens of misapplied ingenuity. So far as
a comparison can be made it would appear that there were
more frauds and forgeries and dishonest uses made of the
Pope's name in that age than have been in subsequent
times of open Protestantism, because in the latter case
defiance took the place of dissimulation.

The Normans may be taken to have been typical of
their age, and hence to have differed both from British
Islanders of the present day and from the Irish of that
day. Differences led to mistakes on all sides, and the
Normans naturally considering their own the best of everything, may be pardoned for holding as barbarous some
Irish practices different from theirs. To take one instance
out of many, the Norman clergy inculcated the payment
of tithes *as a matter of faith*, as anyone who consults their
writings may see. To their minds there could be no more
positive proof of the utter absence of Christianity among
a people than the non-payment of tithes. Ireland, on the
other hand, had passed through her golden age of
Christianity without a State Church, and without paying
tithes. Each clan provided amply for its own clergy, but
in a manner scarcely intelligible to persons unacquainted
with the clan organisation. Benedict, the Abbot of Peter-
borough, writing of the Council of Cashel, says:—" They
also prescribed in that Council that tithes of all they
possessed should be given to ecclesiastics. For the people
generally had never paid tithes, *and did not even know
that they ought to be paid.*"

The justification of the letters now in question is, that
Henry II. of England, shocked at the moral and religious
depravity of the Irish nation, was burning with apostolic
zeal to bring it back to Christian ways, and the temporal
sovereignty of the Western islands having been granted
long ago by Constantine the Great to Pope Sylvester and
his successors, Henry appealed to the Pope to exercise this
hitherto latent sovereignty by appointing him at once Lord

and Second Apostle of Ireland. Lanfranc and St. Anselm, Archbishops of Canterbury, and also St. Bernard, make similar charges of immorality against the Irish of that time. The native Irish annals show but too clearly that the condition of the country was deplorable. The fact was —however a few excellent individuals of Danish race may now endeavour to qualify it—the Danes had well-nigh destroyed Christian civilization in Ireland as well as in England, and had left the tribes of both countries insanely warring against each other—meet prey for the first strong leader at the head of disciplined forces. In religion, in morals, in patriotism, in courage, and in the comforts of private life, the Irish had at that time reached their lowest condition since their conversion from Paganism. Still, the opinions expressed of them by the foreigners mentioned may be due as much to the differences of organisation and method alluded to, and to the consequent misunderstandings, as to real Irish vices. St. Bernard wrote more severely of other people whom he knew than of the Irish whom he did not know. It is now generally conceded that the moral condition of Ireland was by no means so bad as the letters here in question represent. But this does not affect the authenticity of those letters; for whatever may have been Ireland's real condition, it is obvious that then, as now, a tale could be fabricated sufficiently shocking to justify the Pope, and make it his duty, to take action. And if he was informed in the sense indicated in these letters, it would be hard to consider too severe any action he could take.

For the text of the letter bearing Adrian's name, and that of the first bearing Alexander's name, the oldest authority is Giraldus Cambrensis. His contemporaries, Roger de Hovenden and Ralph de Diceto, are also authorities for these two letters, but they add nothing material respecting them. Roger de Wendover and the continuator of his historical works, Matthew Paris, wrote in the following century, and may be taken to have adopted the statements of Giraldus. Matthew Paris inserts Adrian's letter in his *Chronica Majora*, at A.D. 1155, the year in which it purports to have been written. His version of it, so far as it extends, agrees in substance with that of Giraldus; but his arrangement of the sentences is different, and there are two sentences missing. To the letter he prefixes the following note :—

"At that time Henry, king of the English, sending solemn messengers to Rome, asked Pope Adrian to permit him to invade the island of Hibernia with military force, and, extirpating the weeds of vice, to subdue that land, and bring back those bestial people to the faith and the way of truth; Wherefore the Pope, gladly approving of the King's design, accorded to him the following privilege."

In the complete works of Giraldus, published in eight volumes by the Lords Commissioners of the Treasury, and under the direction of the Master of the Rolls, Adrian's privilege occurs three times, namely—in the first, fifth, and eighth volumes. I now submit a literal translation from the eighth volume, and in order to economise space, quote, without a break, the letters of Popes Adrian and Alexander, with the introductory words prefixed to the latter by Giraldus :—

"Adrian, Bishop, servant of the servants of God, to his dearest son in Christ, the illustrious King of the English, greeting and apostolical benediction.

"Your Majesty quite laudably and profitably considers how to extend the glory of your name on earth and increase the reward of eternal happiness in Heaven, when, as a Catholic Prince, you propose to extend the limits of the Church, to announce the truth of the Christian faith to ignorant and barbarous nations, and to root out the weeds of vice from the field of the Lord; and the more effectually to accomplish this you implore the counsel and favour of the Apostolic See. In which matter we are confident that the higher your aim, and the greater the discretion with which you proceed, the happier, with God's help, will be your success; because those things that originate in the

ardour of faith and the love of religion are always wont
to arrive at a good issue and end. Certainly Hibernia and
all the islands upon which Christ the Sun of Justice has
shone, and which have accepted the doctrines of the
Christian faith, of right belong, as your Highness doth
acknowledge, to blessed Peter and the Holy Roman Church.
Wherefore we the more willingly sow in them a faithful
plantation and a seed pleasing to God, in as much as we
know by internal examination that it will be strictly required of us. You have signified to us, dearest son in
Christ, that you desire to enter the island of Hibernia to
subject that people to laws, and to root out therefrom the
weeds of vice; also that you desire to pay from every
house an annual pension of one penny to blessed Peter,
and to preserve the rights of the churches of that land
inviolate and whole. We, therefore, regarding with due
favour your pious and laudable desire, and according a
gracious assent to your petition, deem it pleasing and
acceptable that, for the purpose of extending the limits
of the Church, checking the torrent of wickedness, reforming evil manners, sowing seeds of virtue, and increasing
the Christian religion, you should enter that island and
execute whatever shall be conducive to the honour of God
and the salvation of that land. And let the people of that
land receive you honourably and reverence you as lord,
the rights of the churches remaining indisputably inviolate
and whole, and the annual pension of one penny from
every house being reserved to blessed Peter and the Holy
Roman Church. If, therefore, you will carry to completion
what with a mind so disposed you have conceived, study
to form that people to good morals, and, as well by your-
self as by those whom you shall find qualified for the
purpose by faith, word, and conduct, so act that the Church
may be adorned, that the religion of the Christian faith
may be planted and may increase; and let all that concerns the honour of God and the salvation of souls be
ordered in such manner that you may deserve to obtain
from God a plentiful, everlasting reward, and on earth
succeed in acquiring a name glorious for ages.

"Secundi vero privilegii tenor hic, sicut a quibusdam
impetratum asseritur aut confingitur, ab aliis autem un-
quam impetratum fuisse negatur: *Here, however, is the
tenor of a second privilege, as by some asserted or fabricated
to have been obtained, but by others denied to have ever
been obtained.*

"Alexander, Bishop, servant of the servants of God,

to his dearest son in Christ, the illustrious King of the English, greeting and apostolic benediction.

"In as much as those things which are known to have been introduced, for sufficient reason, by our predecessors ought to be confirmed in permanent stability, we, following in the footsteps of the venerable Pope and expecting the fruition of our own desire, do ratify and confirm his grant over the Hibernian kingdom's dominion bestowed upon you, reserving to blessed Peter and the Holy Roman Church, as well in Hibernia as in England, the annual pension of one penny from every house, so that, the abominations of that land being eradicated, a barbarous nation, which is deemed Christian only in name, may, by your gentle treatment, put on innocence of morals, and, the hitherto undisciplined church of those territories being subjected to discipline, that people may through you henceforth obtain the name and the reality of the Christian profession."

The following three letters do not appear to have been generally known until the eighteenth century. In the second volume of the *Liber Niger Scaccarii*, edited by Thomas Hearne, there are four letters of Pope Alexander III., beginning on page 41. The first of these relates to English affairs, not to Irish; the second is addressed to King Henry II. in relation to his invasion of Ireland; the third, on the same subject, to the Irish princes; the fourth, on the same subject, to the Irish hierarchy. A volume of Migne's *Patrologiæ Cursus* is occupied exclusively with the letters of this Pope, and there also, at the year 1172, these three letters may be seen.

"Alexander, Bishop, servant of the servants of God, to his dearest son in Christ, Henry, the illustrious King of the English, greeting and apostolic benediction.

"We have ascertained from general report and the true relation of many, not without alacrity of mind, how, as a pious king and mighty prince, with the help of the Lord —by whose inspiration, as we verily believe, you have extended your Serenity's power against that rude and undisciplined people—you have wonderfully and magnificently triumphed with respect to that Hibernian nation which, having laid aside the fear of the Lord, wanders as it were unbridled over the precipices of vice, and throws away the restraints of the Christian religion and of virtue, and destroys itself by internecine slaughter, and with respect to that kingdom which the Roman Emperors, conquerors of the world, left, as we have learned, unentered in their own times."

[The writer then says that for the present he will omit mentioning other enormities and vices to which the Irish were addicted, as he had learned from Christian, Bishop of Lismore, the Archbishops and Bishops of Ireland, and Radulphus, Archdeacon of Landaff; and one wonders what the omitted enormities must have been, for a few mentioned are so foul that to reproduce this part of the document here would be an outrage upon the community and would expose one to a criminal prosecution for obscenity. The letter then proceeds]:—

"Wherefore we have learned that, by means of the union of your mighty naval and terrestrial army, you, inspired by divine clemency, have directed your mind to the subjugation of that people to your dominion, and to the extirpation of the filth of so great abominations, as the same archbishops and bishops signify, and the aforesaid archdeacon fully and expressly reports to us, we, as we ought, do hold it by all means pleasing and acceptable. And furthermore we make devout thanksgiving to Him from whom all good proceeds, and Who, in His love of their welfare, disposes the pious acts and wishes of His faithful people. Earnestly beseeching Almighty God with devout prayers that as by the power of your Highness those forbidden things which are done in the country mentioned already begin to desist, and the seeds of virtue to sprout in place of vice, so also, with the help of the Lord, may that nation through you, for an imperishable crown of your eternal glory, and for the progress of its own welfare, having cast off the filth of sins, take on in every respect the discipline of the Christian religion.

"Accordingly we request your Regal Excellence, we charge and exhort you in the Lord, and we enjoin upon you for the remission of your sins, that you stiffen and strengthen your mind still more towards this which you have laudably begun, and by your power call back that nation to, and keep it in, the refinement of the Christian

C

faith; that as, for the obliteration of your sins, you have, as we believe, undertaken such a great work, so also from the progress of its welfare you may merit to obtain an eternal crown.

"And because, like your Highness's excellency, the Roman Church has in an island a right different from what it has in a great and continual land, we holding that hope and confidence from the fervour of your devotion that you desire not only to preserve but even to extend the rights of the Church, and that you ought to establish such a right where none exists, request and earnestly urge upon your Majesty to anxiously study to preserve for us in the beforementioned land the rights of blessed Peter; and if no such rights exist there, let your Highness institute and assign the same to the same Church, so that on this account it may be our duty to return copious thanks to your Royal Highness, and that you may be seen offering the first fruits of your glory and triumph to God."

"Alexander, Bishop, servant of the servants of God, to his beloved children, the distinguished men, petty kings and princes of Hibernia, greeting and apostolical benediction.

"As by common report and the certain relation of many it has become known to us that you have received our dearest son in Christ, Henry, the illustrious king of England, for your king and lord, and have sworn fealty to him, we have felt in our heart a joy so much the greater, as through the power of that king, with the help of the Lord, there will be greater peace and tranquility in your country; and the Hibernian nation, which by the enormity and filth of vice appeared to have receded so very far, will tend more to be informed with divine refinement, and will better receive the discipline of the Christian faith.

"Whence on account of the fact that you have, of your own free will, subjected yourselves to a king so potent and mighty, and a son of the Church so devoted, we watch your prudence with deserved commendation of praise, since from it to yourselves, to the Church, and to all the people of that land, future *advantage not unbounded* (*utilitas non immodica*) may be hoped. We accordingly warn and very earnestly charge your nobility, that the fealty which you have sworn under a religious oath to such a king, you will take care by due submission to keep firm and unshaken: and thus in humility and quietness show yourselves submissive and devoted to him, that you may always receive of him richer favour, and it may be our duty to worthily commend your prudence thereupon."

"Alexander, Bishop, servant of the servants of God, to his venerable brothers in Christ, the Bishop of Lismore, Legate of the Apostolic See, Gelasius of Armagh, Donatus of Cashel, Laurence of Dublin, Catholicus Archbishop of Tuam, and all their suffragans, greeting and apostolic benediction.

"By so great enormities of vice is the Hibernian race infected, and to such an extent are the fear of God and the restraint of the Christian faith set aside, the result, which brings about perils of souls, has been notified to us by a succession of your letters, and no less by the true relation of others also has frequently come to the notice of the Apostolic See.

"Hence it is that we rejoice with gladness as we understand from your letters that by the power of our dearest son in Christ, Henry, the illustrious king of the English, who, moved by divine inspiration, having, by means of his united men, subjected to his dominion that race, barbarous, uncultivated, and ignorant of divine law, those things which were so unlawfully committed in your country already, with God's help, begin to desist. And we heartily offer immense thanksgiving to Him who has conferred so great a victory and triumph upon the king just mentioned. Pray ye humbly beseeching that, by the watchfulness and solicitude of that king, your own care co-operating, that undisciplined and untamed race may by all means and in all things be roused to the refinement of the divine law and the religion of the Christian faith, and that you and other churchmen may rejoice in honour and in meet tranquility.

"Therefore, because it is right that you should manifest anxious watchfulness and favour to the continuance of those things which have commenced with such a pious beginning, we, by apostolic writings, charge and prescribe to your brotherhood, that, as far as you are able, consistently with your order and office, you diligently and manfully assist in subjecting and retaining that land for that renowned king, mighty man, and devoted son of the Church, and in extirpating thence the filth of so great abominations.

"And if any one of the kings, princes, or other men of that land should attempt with daring rashness to violate the obligation of his oath, and his fealty pledged to the aforesaid king, should he not be willing to comply promptly, as he ought to do, with your admonition, let you, relying upon apostolic authority and rejecting every pretext and excuse, assail him with ecclesiastical censure. Let you so diligently and effectually execute our charge, that as the aforesaid king, that Catholic as well as most Christian prince, is said to have piously and kindly hearkened to us in restoring tithes as well as other just ecclesiastical rights to you, and in all those things which appertain to ecclesiastical liberty, so also you should guard firmly those things which relate to the royal dignity, and, as far as in you lies, cause others to guard them."

CHAPTER II.

John of Salisbury and the Evidence attributed to him.

THE document given under Adrian's name, commonly called the Bull *Laudabiliter*, bears, as we shall see, a striking resemblance to a Bull of Adrian's that is unquestionably genuine. It is the letter which the subsequent letter under Alexander's name purports to confirm. It is the letter mentioned by English historical writers in the twelfth and thirteenth centuries, and quoted by some of them. It is the letter upon which the title of Lord of Ireland rested until the Reformation. It is the letter the authenticity of which has been recognised by two Popes, and by an Irish remonstrance addressed to one of them. It finds a place in the *Annales Ecclesiastici* of Cardinal Baronius, in one edition of the *Bullarium*, and in Migne's collection. All this, as stated, constitutes a *prima facie* case of such overwhelming force as to amply justify our inquiry, and accounts for one gentleman exclaiming that there is not a better authenticated fact in the domain of history. Indeed to question the authenticity of documents so supported makes some knowing ones shake their heads; and, on the suggestion of their spuriousness, a writer whose blushes must here be spared asks naively in the *Irish Ecclesiastical Record* for February, 1893, " could it be possible?" The answer to this question is supplied in the sentence with which Giraldus Cambrensis introduces the first letter under Pope Alexander's name. In that sentence the letter is described as one which may have been fabricated (or pretended) to have been obtained. Hereby the whole case is given away, and the possibility and probability of forgery are admitted by this the very earliest authority for the text of these alleged Papal letters.

The latest Editor of the *De Principis Instructione*, in which this destructive sentence is prefixed to Alexander's letter, neither offers a word of comment nor directs his readers' attention to that sentence; though, striking as it does at the authenticity of the letter, it is clearly of vital importance. Had the letter purported to tamper with, let us say, the freedom of England, no passage in all Giraldus's works would have been subjected to closer scrutiny than this sentence, and no editor would have ventured to pass it over in silence, except at the risk of his reputation. Some who maintain that these letters are authentic similarly ignore this sentence, and withhold from their readers the knowledge of its existence, thereby involuntarily admitting its force. But there it stands in black and white, refusing to disappear on being ignored. When confronted with it they take refuge in the allegation, without any reason, that it is spurious. As if by way of concession to them, and to his own inclination, Mr. Dimock says in another place that it may have been originally a marginal note. By whom? or wherefore made? It stands not on the margin but in the text of the oldest existing manuscript copies: and there is no reason except its inconvenience for suggesting that it ever stood anywhere else. And supposing that it did stand on the margin, it might have been placed there by Giraldus in obedience to a prick of conscience. The next most likely person to place it there would be a monk at St. Alban's, where the work was copied. In either case its force would not be in any degree weakened, but rather strengthened, for it would be a record of the cool and dispassionate doubt of an Englishman naturally pre-disposed to maintain the authenticity of the letters unless he saw grave reason for doubting. But our immediate point is, that the sentence gives an affirmative answer to the question: Could forgery in such a case be possible?

What purports to be the oldest authority for the letter given under Adrian's name, and what is ultimately the most difficult to shake, is a passage at the end of a work called the *Metalogicus*, written by John of Salisbury, a very learned priest and polished courtier, who afterwards became Bishop of Chartres. The work is undoubtedly his, and was written about 1159; but the authenticity of this particular passage at the end of it has been questioned.

We now approach the most crucial point in our discussion, and if we would solve the riddle before us it is absolutely necessary to study this man and this writing very narrowly. We shall have to deal with characters as interesting, but with none so important. It has been suggested that John's character was not above suspicion, that he may have written the passage in the *Metalogicus* fraudulently and falsely at the bidding of King Henry, and that the bishopric of Chartres may have been his reward for so doing. I believe it will be more correct, as well as more pleasant, to reject this odious supposition and proceed on the assumption that John was an honourable man and, therefore, incapable of acting in the manner suggested. I will present the man and the writing as fairly as space will permit:—

John was born at Old Sarum (Salisbury) between 1115 and 1120. In his youth, before 1130, he went to Paris to study, and he did not return to England until 1150, that is to say, for more than twenty years. It is thought that during part of this time he obtained a living and the means of pursuing his studies by writing letters and transacting kindred business for various persons. From 1150 until 1164, excepting some visits to the Continent, he lived at the Archiepiscopal Court of Canterbury. Some political and judicial as well as ecclesiastical business was transacted there, and John appears to have discharged the duties of secretary, to some extent, for two successive Archbishops, Theobald and Thomas à Becket. In 1164 he left England, and both he and Becket spent some years in exile, returning to England in 1170 when King Henry's wrath seemed to be appeased. John was present at Canterbury, and counselled prudence, when the murderers of Becket were expected. When they appeared he ran away. In 1176 he was made Bishop of Chartres, the chapter of the diocese having elected him unanimously. Whether this was their own spontaneous action or the result of the nomination of some higher power, does not appear. John died at Chartres in 1180. Thus, though he took from his birth-place the surname by which he was best known, he spent the greater part of his life on the Continent. The effect of this may be seen in his language and sentiments, which are more French or Roman than English. His "Constantinus noster" and many other expressions are not at all suggestive of a British Islander. He was a warm supporter of the Pope's temporal power. He wrote very graceful Latin, and in classical learning was scarcely equalled by any man of his age. Most of his writings are those of a mild-mannered man, and they contain many passages indicative of his modesty; but that he could be peevish is evidenced by his calling the Archbishop of York an archdevil. A man of his learning and experience must have been quite conscious of his capacity. While there was probably some sincerity, there may also have been a little affectation, in his extending the meaning of *Parvus*, which, on account of his smallness of stature, had become affixed to him as a surname, and describing himself as "parvum nomine, facultate minorem, minimum merito."

With a view to the present discussion I have sought at the Lambeth Palace Library and at the British Museum for the author's manuscript of the *Metalogicus*, and have learned that no such thing exists. I have examined the manuscripts of it that do exist. There is nothing in them to show positively when or by whom they were written; but at both the beginning and the end of them it is intimated in red ink that they are copies of writings of John of Salisbury, who was afterwards Bishop of Chartres. Judging by the illuminated initial letters one would say they were probably written in the fourteenth century. These very manuscripts may have been the sources of the printed editions, from which they do not differ materially.

Since we cannot apply the test of handwriting, it becomes important in order to judge of the congruity of the passage in question, to know the subject and general tenor of the work, the author's usual method, the position this passage occupies in the work, and the precise words of the passage.

The work is an interesting one, in which the bitter is blended with the sweet in a manner suggestive of Swift. It is divided into four books, each consisting of a number of short chapters. There is an order and sequence among the chapters, while at the same time they are so written that they might stand as separate essays on their respective subjects. The opening chapter of the work is a character sketch, the name of the subject not being given. Then follow chapters more or less abstract, on reason and morality. From these the author passes to the praise of eloquence, and afterwards to the praise of exercise. He then makes a defence of the study of logic; after which he seems to turn away to discuss the liberal arts, poetry, art in general, and devotes a few chapters to grammatical subjects. In these chapters the author gives incidentally many glimpses of his student years, nor does he in any of them wholly lose sight of his main subject, which is a discussion of the limits of logic and a defence of its study. But the first book is rather introductory and discursive. The second book opens with the proposition that "logic, since it seeks what is true, is serviceable to all wisdom." From this opening the work is steadily logical, philosophical, and learned.

As the fourth book of the *Metalogicus* stands at present, there are in it forty-two chapters, the forty-second being that with which we are concerned. Its position at the end is obviously more favourable than any other position in the work for the subsequent introduction of matter by the author or by any other person. Anything so written at the end would be strictly an addition, not an interpolation. The forty-first chapter ends with a consideration of eight obstacles of the understanding. The work might very properly have ended with this chapter. In fact, the subject is ended, for chapter forty-two contains nothing relevant to it, and the following is the beginning of the chapter, so far as it is material for us:—

"But these things so far. For now is a time to weep rather than to write: and by visible proof I am taught that the whole world is subject to vanity. For we expected peace, and behold a disturbance and storm, bursting upon the people of Tolosa, excites the English and Gauls everywhere. And kings, whom we have seen as dearest friends, pursue each other insatiably. Besides, the death of our lord Adrian, the supreme pontiff, while it has afflicted all peoples and nations of the Christian religion, has moved with a more bitter sorrow our own England whence he was sprung, and has watered her with more profuse tears. Upon all the good a doleful sorrow has fallen, but upon none more doleful than upon me. For although he had a mother and a uterine brother, he loved me with a warmer affection than them. He admitted both publicly and privately that he loved me beyond all mortals. He had conceived such an esteem for me that, as often as opportunity offered, he delighted to pour out his conscience in my sight. And when he had become Roman Pontiff he was pleased to have my company at his own table, and he wished the same cup and plate to serve us both, and us to live in common, a thing I resisted. At my entreaties he granted and gave to the illustrious King of the English, Henry the Second, Hibernia, to be held by hereditary right, as his own letter testifies to the present day. For all islands are said to belong by an ancient right to the Roman Church, in virtue of the donation of Constantine, who founded and endowed it. He also sent by me a gold ring, adorned with a choice emerald, wherewith an investiture of the right of governing Hibernia should take place, and hitherto this ring has been ordered to be kept in the public archives. . . ."

It will be seen that this is quite foreign to the subject with which chapter forty-one closed. Although in itself natural enough, here it seems incongruous and out of place. It might, therefore, be readily stamped as spurious if the *Metalogicus* were the work of a writer of strictly logical methods. But those who on the ground of incongruity brand this chapter as spurious, do not appear to me to have studied John of Salisbury. Although he wrote on logic, he resembled a great many people in not always practising what he preached: and although the matter of this chapter is irrelevant to the work to which it is appended, I am unable to pronounce it on that ground alone wholly inconsistent with John's character. Nor is there anything in the style to arouse suspicion. Let us examine the terms of the passage and compare them with those of the instrument to which they are said to refer. It is unfortunate for that instrument that this passage quoted from the end of the *Metalogicus*, the most venerable evidence in support of its authenticity, itself bears ostentatious and conclusive evidence of the possibility of forgery. The quotation actually embodies a classic forgery of precisely the same order as the one whose possibility is here in question. In naming Constantine's donation as the foundation of this privilege and the source of the power in virtue of which it was granted, the writer in the *Metalogicus* settles the doubt of possibility by reminding us of one of the most elaborate and successful forgeries in history.

Some time probably in the ninth century, copies of a document were put in circulation purporting to be a privilege of the Emperor Constantine the Great, made a few days after his baptism, and conferring on Pope

Sylvester and his successors the Imperial palaces, the Imperial insignia, and lands in Asia, Africa, and Europe, especially the western islands. It gained credence, and in the course of the eleventh century found its way into learned works and into the Canon Law, where it may be seen to this day embedded, like a fly in amber, in the standard digest of Canon Law by Gratianus, which has been read for centuries in the schools and universities of Europe. It seems to have been considered genuine throughout the greater part of Christendom. It was believed in by several Popes, and by them made the foundation of Bulls, letters, and various proceedings; and it was cited in sermons. In the sixteenth century Cardinal Baronius and other grappled with it, and pronounced it spurious. Further research since then has confirmed their view, and now the so-called privilege of Constantine is universally known to have been an elaborate imposture. Its present discredit, however, does not disturb its mediæval credit and potency. These it could never have acquired had it not been concocted by a learned and clever man, and by him skilfully fitted to the facts and persons of the time to which it purported to belong. To succeed, it required much more than the bare writing of the document. Its success proves that its author was no dunce. That success at the centre of Christianity and in the face of learned Europe, removes all doubt with respect to the easier task of floating a spurious Papal Bull relating to a remote island. The text of the Imperial privilege and that of several other questionable documents may be seen in the writings of Gratianus, and also in the *Corpus Juris Canonici, Decreti Pars Prima, Distinctio XCVI.*, c. 14. The following are the passages construed to include Ireland :—

"1. Ecclesiis beatorum apostolorum Petri et Pauli pro continuatione luminariorum possessionum predia contulimus, et rebus diversis eas ditavimus, et per nostram imperialem jussionem sacram tam in oriente, *quam in occidente, vel etiam septentrionali* et meridiana plaga, videlicet in Judea, Grecia, Asia, Thracia, Affrica, et Italia, *vel diversis insulis*, nostra largitate ei concessimus, ea prorsus ratione, ut per manus beatissimi patris nostri Silvestri summi Pontificis successorumque ejus omnia disponantur.

. . . .

"6. Unde ut pontificalis apex non vilescat, sed magis quam terreni imperii dignitas gloria et potentia decoretur, ecce tam palatium nostrum, ut prædictum est, quam Romanam urbem, et omnes Italiae *seu occidentalium regionum* provincias, loca et civitates præfato beatissimo Pontifici nostro Silvestro universali Papae contradimus atque relinquimus, et ab eo et a successoribus ejus per hanc divalem nostram et pragmaticum constitutum decernimus disponenda atque juri sanctae Romanae ecclesiae concedimus permansura."

The Imperial privilege ends by fervently consigning to eternal perdition all who should dare to resist it.

In his *Ecclesiastical History*, vol. iv., page 160, Dr. Lanigan says:—"This nonsense about the Pope's being head owner of all Christian islands had been partially announced to the world in a Bull of Urban II., in 1091." It had, however, been announced as early as 1054; but the announcement of Urban II. was more distinct and agressive, and did not look as if he considered it nonsense. The following are the words used in a Bull granting the Liparian Islands to the monastery of St. Bartholomew:—

"Cum universae insulae secundum instituta regalis juris sint, constat profecto quia religiosi imperatoris Constantini privilegio in jus proprium beato Petro ejusque successoribus occidentales omnes insulae condonatae sunt, maxime quae circa Italiae oram habentur."

After Urban II. no Pope appears to have made any use of or reference to the supposed Imperial privilege for more than a hundred years. It was not used by any Pope in the twelfth century, the century with which we are concerned. In the thirteenth century it was relied upon by Innocent III. and Gregory IX.; in the fourteenth century by John

XXII.; in the fifteenth century by Nicholas V., Calixtus III., Sixtus IV., and Alexander VI. The foregoing being all the known instances of Papal reliance on Constantine's donation, one wonders why so little use was made of an instrument promising so much. Only one Pope used it in a way that could be called rapacious. By the others named it was used sparingly, diffidently, or only by way of example; and even at the time of its greatest vogue the larger number of Popes do not appear to have mentioned it at all. Whether this was due to want of faith in it, or to the difficulty of realising the gift, or to reluctance, or to indifference, must now remain matter of opinion. Although the temporal power of the Pope may have derived some advantage from the spurious Imperial donation, it was not to any appreciable extent due to that instrument, but was in part assumed by the Popes in their pontifical character, in part conferred on them by princes and peoples themselves; and being based on the pastoral relation to human souls, it necessarily affected, without distinction, continents as well as islands. Hence the weakness of the claim, in so far as it rested upon Constantine, consisted not in its extent, but rather in its limitation to islands.

The possibility of forgery being easy, an example being at hand, and suspicion not being modern but as old as the letters themselves, and coming down to us from the same authority, and, moreover, the case being one in which no decisive fact of direct import can be established on either side, we are not merely justified but bound to inquire what the truth of the case is, to test and check matters and persons in every way now open to us, to turn facts and assertions inside out, and submit them to reason, to balance probabilities point by point as we proceed, and thus to glean all the truth they will yield, whatever its tendency. Alike those who accept and those who reject the Bulls in question will, if sincere, court the closest scrutiny of them. For, if those documents are authentic, close examination will make their authenticity more manifest, and by elucidating strengthen every point that has hitherto been weak or doubtful. While, on the other hand, if they should fail to bear this test, if light or inspection should reveal any falsehood or inconsistency in them, it will be our duty to follow the clue, and a good deed to expose what is false and has been too long accepted as true. The facts being connected chain-like, the destruction of one link would imperil the whole.

The last chapter of the *Metalogicus* proceeds to say that the Papal letter just described had been preserved in the royal archives, Winchester Castle " to the present day " [ad hodiernum]. This expression, in so far as it suggests that a considerable time had elapsed since the letter had been written, is inconsistent with this chapter having been written so early as 1159, the date at which it should have been written to be genuine. On the other hand, if this chapter was written a number of years later, and, therefore, illegitimately, a considerable time having then, in fact, elapsed, the writer would be peculiarly liable to say so, that being then the natural thing to say, and, in one sense, favourable to his purpose.

A warm admirer of John of Salisbury's learning and character says, " Henry, who asked the privilege, and the Pope who granted it, believed in Constantine's donation." Observe the clearness, completeness and conclusiveness of this assertion as it stands. But does it stand? Where is the authority for it? There is absolutely none. Neither of the personages named has left a word to show whether he believed in Constantine's donation or not. The vigorous assertion wholly lacks confirmation. The more John of Salisbury is credited with learning the less probable becomes his belief in Constantine's donation ; and we cannot, with any regard for his moral character, suppose that he made use of it knowing it to be spurious. His learning also discredits the assumption of the writer in the *Meta-*

logicus that Ireland had belonged to Constantine, and was in his gift. He had a special knowledge of Roman Law, under which strangers acquired prescriptive ownership of property by possession continued for a number of years, and, therefore, he could not possibly have imagined that the Irish people had lost prescriptive ownership of their own country by possession continued for many centuries. Hence, to maintain that he wrote the last chapter in the *Metalogicus* amounts to assailing his reputation for learning and his moral character.

The Bull *Laudabiliter* never having been proved, and it being utterly impossible to prove anything affirmative with respect to it, the conjecture that it is the document referred to by the writer in the *Metalogicus* may be incorrect. As it is generally accepted, especially by those who maintain the authenticity of the Bull, the discussion is best restricted by our accepting the conjecture. As we proceed comparing the terms of the letter with those of the writing in the *Metalogicus*, and find it becoming more and more clear that they are absolutely irreconcilable with each other, the thought will spring up involuntarily that perhaps the writing refers to some wholly different letter. It will be well to remember, on each such occasion of difficulty in this one direction, that in the alternative direction the difficulties are as numerous and formidable.

To what Papal letter does the passage at the end of the *Metalogicus* relate? By general consent to the *Laudabiliter*. But that is a document addressed by a Pope Adrian not specified to a King of England not named; and the brief which purports to confirm it is in the same indefinite condition. There can, therefore, be no certainty of identification; we cannot be sure that we have before us the instrument meant by the writer in the *Metalogicus*; and in addition to this, the instrument we have before us is not in the usual form of a Papal Bull. That this latter is not at all a trifling difficulty anyone may learn on looking into the *Bullarium* and seeing there the letters of these two Popes, addressed at the beginning to individuals by name, and at the end specifying the particular Pope, with the name of the Papal Chancellor by whose hands they were delivered. We shall have to deal later with an argument that these letters were written in pursuance of a common form, and mention it here only for the purpose of remarking that the most common of all forms was to address individuals by name, and to conclude Papal letters as stated. In no other letter of these two Popes that is given in full in the *Bullarium*, are these two common forms departed from. It is as certain as anything can be that the Papal scribes who were accustomed to write so carefully and formally for Adrian and Alexander did not, on these two occasions only, lapse so sadly as to write these letters in the condition in which we find them—a condition which has been correctly described as being "without head or tail." Had they been so written, no chancellor would sign or issue documents of their purport in such an unusual and imperfect condition. To whatever cause or misfortune the loss may be due, these marks of authenticity are absent from the more important of the letters we are considering; and their imperfect condition, so far from being trifling, renders their identification and their authentication alike impossible, and is, therefore, fatal to their negotiability. It is beyond the power of man to prove that the *Laudabiliter* is the letter referred to in the *Metalogicus*. It is beyond the power of man to prove that it is a genuine Papal letter. The plea that these omissions occurred in transcription goes but a short way. From the beginning to the present day these letters have been copied thus; while from the beginning to the present day other Papal letters, that have been copied as often, have still retained their marks of authenticity. To say that a thing was deemed worth preserving as a State Paper in Winchester Castle and then to offer as an excuse that it was not deemed worth copying correctly, is a manifest contradiction. The conclusion therefore is, that the first and second of the Bulls in question have in fact always been copied as originally written; and all that deters people from frankly accepting this reasonable conclusion is the obvious consequence that then the originals could not have been genuine.

Another obstacle to the identification of the same two Bulls is the absence of time or place of delivery. It may be thought that this adaptable condition is convenient, as it permits of their being fitted by reasoners into the most sheltered corner. But this is a convenience attended with some risk. The importance of a date being universally recognised, one is sometimes appended, and it is "*given at Rome,*" etc. Things Papal being usually Roman, things purporting to be Papal are so fitted in the matter of date as not to disappoint a common expectation. But to this considerate arrangement the discovery is disastrous that the Pope did not reside at Rome at the time that either one or the other of them should have been written to be genuine.

A date has also a use besides assisting in identification. Its date is a material part of a document, and the affixing, erasing, or altering of it by an unauthorised person constitutes forgery. The fact of the date of an instrument having been tampered with is conclusive proof that those in whose custody it has been have had an interest in it different from the interest of truth, and have not scrupled to alter it in favour of that interest. Such tampering wholly vitiates and invalidates it in their hands and renders inadmissible, except of grace, any evidence such persons might desire to offer regarding it or any document connected with it. A person who would alter the date of an instrument to suit a purpose would have as little scruple in writing the whole instrument, or as many of the sort as his purpose required.

The *Laudabiliter* differs from genuine Bulls of the

period, in bearing neither the name of him to whom it is alleged to have been addressed, nor the names of those who on Henry's behalf are said to have obtained it, nor the signature of the Pope at the end to specify which Adrian issued it, nor the signature of the Papal chancellor, nor the place whence it was issued, nor the month, nor the year of Christ, nor the year of Adrian's pontificate. If the absence of any one of these particulars might raise a question of authenticity, the absence of them all seems to leave little trace of authenticity to be looked for.

The *Laudabiliter* itself says explicitly that it was granted at the request of the King. The writer in the *Metalogicus* says as explicitly that he obtained it at his own request [ad preces meas]. Let supporters of the letters reconcile these two contradictory statements if they can. Anyone who examines the writings of John of Salisbury will readily concede that he was quite incapable of such a wanton breach of taste, prudence and truth as this statement would be if the favour had been obtained at the request of the King. Indeed it is obvious that in a semi-political matter he was a man much more likely to attribute undue merit to his King than to detract merit that was really due to the King, and appropriate it to himself. On the other hand, did any Pope ever transfer, or attempt to transfer, the dominion of one country to the king of another, on the entreaty of a private individual, without being asked by the king about to be favoured, and without consulting the nation about to be affected? Never. Yet mark, the writer who has the incredible conceit to claim that he, by his own entreaties, accomplished this extraordinary feat, is, we are asked to believe, the same who describes himself as *Johannes Minimus Merito*.

The statements in the *Metalogicus* are couched, with such skill veiled as simplicity, in what seems to be a natural and spontaneous expression of the writer's thoughts, that on the first reading, although one feels that there is something wrong, he gives a reluctant assent, not knowing where the defect lies. Just turn back to the passage quoted and judge if the familiarity with the Pope was not somewhat excessive. Read how the Pope loved John better than he loved his mother and brother. Read the climax, how the Pope declared publicly and privately that he loved John beyond all mortals. Consider whether this is not overdone. Then consider whether it is not like a vigorous invention to prepare the reader to accept the still more astounding statement that *at this man's request* the Pope had made a present of Ireland to the King of England. Further, conceive the same Pope there and then dictating a Bull to the effect that he was giving this same favour *at the King's request*. Behold! Finally, turn to Giraldus, Hovenden, Wendover, Matthew Paris, and other old writers who mention the Bull and you will find them stating that it was granted at the King's request, of which a solemn embassy consisting of three bishops and the Abbot of St. Albans are said to have been the bearers. More astonishing still, all these conflicting accounts of how the Bull was obtained are now put forward *by the same writers*, but at such distances apart that a casual reader may have forgotten one theory before he has reached its rival. When the theories are gathered together in a handy bundle as here, the impossibility of all of them being true becomes so obvious that one naturally asks if any one of them is true, and feels tempted to throw the bundle into the fire. In truth, all of them are assailable; but here we must confine ourselves to the claim made in John's name, and we have found it to be irreconcilable alike with his character and with the letter to be authenticated.

The letter purports to confer rights and powers of which the writer himself, as Pontiff, was the source. The writer in the *Metalogicus* speaks of a letter conferring temporal ownership in virtue of a power derived from Constantine the Great. The letter claims in a vague manner for the

Roman Church, but does not transfer to Henry, all islands upon which Christ, the Sun of Justice, has shone. This extensive claim is not, and obviously could not have been, based on the supposed donation of Constantine. The writer does not say what the basis of the claim is. Whence the power was supposed to be derived is in itself immaterial to us. We are only concerned to observe that the letter and the chapter contradict each other with regard to the source of the power, as they do upon other points, and that the letter does no purport to transfer any right of ownership, while the chapter says it does.

The writer of the letter and the writer in the *Metalogicus* speak of rights that are essentially different. The letter is entirely devoted to spiritul matters, religious and moral. Spiritual motives are the only ones manifested in it. It is only for spiritual purposes that it approves of Henry's going to Ireland, and the rights and powers which it purports to confer on him are spiritual, and intended for those purposes. In extent they are limited only by Henry's own notion of what the case required. Practically that means unlimited. They are, therefore, more extensive than the powers conferred on any Papal Legate. The letter approves of his entering the country, to extend the limits of the Church, to announce the truth of the Christian faith, to root out the weeds of vice from the field of the Lord, to check the torrent of wickedness, to reform evil manners, to sow seeds of virtue, to increase the Christian religion, and to execute whatever should be conducive to the glory of God and the salvation of that land; and it goes beyond all this by assuring Henry that the higher his aims the happier would be his success. All these were very excellent purposes if needed, and the power to effect them would have been well bestowed on a suitable person. No doubt it becomes somewhat startling when we reflect that to do all this the Pope must have ignored or superseded his own Legate then in Ireland and the whole Irish

Hierarchy, and without consulting them, placed this wilful young layman over their heads—a spiritual autocrat, armed with unlimited spiritual powers. But this inherent improbability must be dealt with later, and is not the point of this paragraph. Extensive though the range of approval is, it includes nothing which did not belong to the Papal office. Its bestowal would neither have transferred sovereignty nor conveyed seisin, nor in any way constituted Adrian a donor of other people's property. No learned man, least of all John of Salisbury, would mistake them for a hereditary right to possess the country. Few men of his time, if any, knew the difference between spiritual and temporal rights better than did John of Salisbury. To mark and maintain the distinction between them was one of the duties of his life. To confuse them or mistake one for the other was a species of blunder not to be attributed to any learned man, but least of all to him. He was guarded from it by his learning, by his mode of life, and by this additional and peculiar fact that if he had obtained the letter by his own prayers he would have known better than anyone else what its contents and purport were.

We have no difficulty in believing that the acquisition of both a hereditary right to possess the country and ecclesiastical omnipotence in the country would have been very acceptable to Henry, and that both the letter and the chapter in the *Metalogicus*, while irreconcilable with each other, quite harmonized with his views. Is not this harmony suspicious and suggestive? The *Laudabiliter* purported to confer upon Henry unlimited ecclesiastical power. The *Metalogicus* purported to confer upon him unlimited temporal power. These were just the things to acquire which was the object of his whole policy in England. No gift could be more complete. Nothing more remained to be given. Than both together, nothing could be more comprehensive, nothing more agreeable to Henry, or more in accordance with his ambition. If both were written by sycophants in his own palace, and at his own dictation, they could not have more fully gratified his desires. So far as regarded the matter of them, he could not be expected to quarrel with either; and he would naturally trust to others to make them reconcilable with each other, and otherwise presentable. The most consistent policy of Henry's life was to maintain that spiritual and temporal power were alike inseparable parts of the royal prerogative, that the Church was a department of the State, and that to him as head of the State belonged the property and rights of the Church, including the right to appoint its officers, its bishops and clergy. The position of the Church in his dominions gave frequent occasion for his assumptions; for if it had the strength it had also the weakness incidental to a State Church. One of the commonest of these is the inevitable tendency of individual clergymen of such a Church to look for promotion to livings, not as a reward of good work among the people, but as a result of intrigue. Henry was courted for favours, which, like Pilate, he should never have had the power to bestow. He sometimes kept sees vacant for a time, and thus had the double pleasure of enjoying their revenues and homage of the candidates for them. The relations between the Church and him were continually strained, and his conduct was the cause of most of the troubles. The policy of the Church, so far from being one of slavish acquiescence, as these letters would convey, was one of consistent resistance. St. Thomas of Canterbury, in a letter to Pope Alexander III., complains that Henry was improperly assuming that dominion over the Church of England was his "*by hereditary right.*" Pope Alexander III. writes to Henry, under date 9th October, 1167, a long letter, crammed from beginning to end with complaints, warnings, and threats. He directly accuses Henry of being another Cæsar, and worse than Cæsar, since he unlawfully and to the peril of his soul dares to usurp, not merely the things which belong to Cæsar, but those also which belong to God. He tells Henry that his conduct is unworthy of a king and contrary to royal justice; and adjures him, in the name of the Lord, to change his ways, for the sake of the Church and for the remission of his sins. This was strong language to address to such a man, as strong as could be used without an utter breach, as strong as the most advanced democrat of the present day could desire. It would be easy to cite other letters and documents to the same effect, all written —mark well—*before* Henry's character had been stained by the murder of Beckett. When the ominous struggle between Henry and Thomas à Becket had been brought to a close, and Thomas had returned from exile to Canterbury, Pope Alexander wrote a congratulatory letter to Henry, on what then appeared to be the happy termination of the struggle and the restoration of peace. If this Pontiff had been addicted to that fulsome flattery, with which these letters relating to Ireland teem, this was a tempting and pardonable occasion for giving way to that weakness. The Pope does nothing of the sort, relinquishes not an iota of the rights of the Church, but insists upon the last farthing, so to speak, and writes a letter worthy of his office and of himself. Power of every kind, and hereditary right, were things dear to Henry's heart, documents conferring all of them were certain to please him, but he knew better than to look to the Pope for them.

The letter and the passage in the *Metalogicus* being in obstinate disagreement, a desperate attempt is made to bridge the chasm at this point by suggesting that the phrase "hereditary right" in the latter was justified by the petition for the privilege rather than by the privilege itself, and that the petition was written by John of Salisbury, and was therefore in his mind. The architect of this fantastic bridge had better not take his stand upon it. He describes John as "morally and intellectually one of

the most imposing figures of the thirteenth century." John
of Salisbury had been dead twenty years before the
thirteenth century began. But overlooking that fact, this
remains, that if he presented a petition for a hereditary
right to possess Ireland, he failed to obtain that right, yet
here he is represented as expressly stating that he had obtained it, and by his own prayers. This seems to leave his
moral figure in rather a bad plight.

John of Salisbury was a prolific writer for that age. A
collection of his works in prose and verse may be seen in
Migne's volumes. Although they deal with a great variety
of subjects and show their author to have been communicative, they do not contain a word in confirmation of either
the *Laudabiliter* or the passage in the *Metalogicus*. We
need not consider his poetry or his works on distinctly religious subjects, in which these matters have obviously no
place. But his letters are numerous, constituting the
largest portion of his writings, and so full of anecdotes and
reminiscences that a biography of him might be compiled
from them. From writing letters for other people he
took to writing for himself; and 339 of his letters, preserved in Migne's collection, are spoken of as few, so many
did he write. Some of these, however, were written in the
name of the Archbishop of Canterbury; but the greater
number by far were written in his own name, and in all
the language, the sentiments, the literary and autobiographical flavour are clearly his own. Rev. W. B. Morris
when pursuing the same inquiry in which we are engaged
said to himself, very naturally, if John of Salisbury had
this Bull so much on his mind that he could not keep it
out of a treatise on Aristotle and Logic, surely he will
mention it to the persons concerned and to his intimate
friends. Father Morris thereupon examined all these
letters, and although the collection contains twenty-seven
letters addressed to Pope Adrian, eleven to King Henry II.,
and twenty-three to Pope Alexander, extending over the

years from 1155 to 1180, and some of them relating to subjects in which mention of the privilege, if it existed, would have been germane and in order, there is no such mention nor anything that could be construed as such. This is, indeed, negative evidence, but of such cogency that it is scarcely necessary to point the moral. It reduces us to a choice of two propositions: Either (*a*) this communicative man, who is said to have been so anxious in 1155 about the condition of Ireland, wrote all those letters during all those years without once mentioning that object of his anxiety, and wrote to the persons who are alleged to have been concerned in this privilege, and to others, without once mentioning that he had procured it, a thing which if true, would have been fair matter for boast, and vastly more important than many things he writes about; or (*b*) his silence, otherwise unaccountable, is satisfactorily explained by his not knowing any of these things, never having obtained the privilege or heard of its existence, and never having written the last chapter now in the *Metalogicus*. Of these two propositions which is the more probable? Only one answer is possible. Add to this the fact that while the latter proposition would simplify the whole case, the former would leave it for ever perplexed.

The letters furnish more than this strong negative evidence. If John of Salisbury be accepted as a witness in his own defence, his letters furnish positive evidence of the most striking and apt character that his writings were tampered with, that liberties were taken with his name in his own time, and that all writings bearing his name are not his. His letter, numbered 61, is addressed to King Henry in answer to an inquiry regarding certain letters which had reached Henry, purporting to have been written by John of Salisbury, and complaining that the writer had been passed over while one less entitled had obtained ecclesiastical promotion. Nothing could look more plausible and genuine, nothing more unassailable, than letters of that class written to the King at a time when promotion would have been acceptable to John. Were they authentic? John's answer is an indignant and spirited denial that he had written such letters. His tone may be gathered from this extract: —

" Ecce, Domino inspectore et judice, loquar in auribus vestris quod verum est. Litteras istas nec scripsi, nec scribere volui, nec ab aliquo meorum scriptas novi. Falsae sunt, et eis ad delusionem vestram, et sui damnationem solus falsarius scienter usus est."

After his letters, our author's largest work is the *Policraticus* (=Statesman's Book), described by way of subtitle as a treatise *de Nugis Curialium et Vestigiis Philosophorum*. These names being appropriate, it will be understood that the work is extensive and its limits elastic. It is a work nearly three times as large as the *Metalogicus*, and occupies about seven hundred small octavo pages. It is divided into eight books, each made up of short chapters. These are like so many separate essays. In some cases their arrangement shows their relation to each other; in parts they do not appear to have been arranged but only mixed. They run over a variety of subjects—religious, moral, philosophical, literary, musical, historical, and political, most of them having some bearing on or relation to the court politics of the author's time, and some chapters being expressly devoted to current politics. In short, it is a collection of congenial studies for a statesman of the twelfth century, relieved by lighter matter.

The sixth book of this work is taken up mainly with the application of moral and religious rules to the military profession, and some illustrations are drawn from recent and current English affairs. A tribute is paid to Henry II. for having calmed the storm raised by Stephen, and pacified the island. This book would have been a most appropriate place in which to mention the privilege we are discussing, or anything else of that character. Its suitability becomes still more obvious when we read in the twenty-fourth chapter of this book the following words: —

"I remember an occasion of visiting, away in Apulia, our lord, the Pontiff, Adrian the Fourth, who admitted me to the utmost familiarity; and I tarried almost three months with him at Beneventum. When accordingly, as is usual among friends, we often chatted about many things, and he inquired familiarly and diligently from me what people thought regarding himself and the Roman Church, I, employing freedom of spirit, laid frankly before him the evil things which I had heard in divers provinces. For, as was said by many, the Roman Church, which is the mother of all churches, shows herself not so much a mother as a stepmother."

He proceeds to give the substance of his free conversations with the Pope and many details of what passed between them. In it all there is nothing unseemly or improbable, nothing about using the same cup and plate, nothing about loving John beyond all mortals, and alas for our privilege *there is not a word about it.* Yet those who maintain that it is genuine assure us that this was the occasion on which it was obtained, and that to obtain it was the special object of this visit, the special purpose for which John had been sent to the Pope. It is also presumably the occasion referred to in the *Metalogicus.* Why then are we not told of the privilege here, where the statement would have been germane to the matter in hand, almost a duty, almost an essential part of the record? How can the omission be accounted for? We are offered two explanations: first, that Henry for some political reason desired the privilege to be kept a secret; secondly, that it was of no importance, not worth mentioning. If these explanations are sound they will bear examination.

With regard to explanation number one: Both the *Policraticus* and the *Metalogicus* were finished in Henry's dominions in 1159. If the last chapter in the *Metalogicus* was written then and by the same writer, as it expressly purports it to have been—at the date of the siege of Toulouse—how was the King's secret kept? Again, the same persons who allege this desire of Henry to keep the privilege secret tell us that it was discussed in 1156 at an assembly of notables, and that Henry was dissuaded by his mother and the Saxons from putting it in force. For this statement they refer to Robert de Monte. Feeble though his support would be, he does not give it to the alleged Bulls ; he does not say they were discussed ; he makes no mention whatsoever of them, and gives no reason for supposing that he ever heard of them. The discussion, the dissuasion, and the King's secret are alike imaginary and ridiculous. If not, how did a matter discussed in an assembly in 1156 become a secret three years later, and such a curious secret, too, that the principal actor was free to mention it in a book with which it had no connection whatever, but dared not mention it in the book of which, if true, it should properly have formed a part? The most plausible reason alleged for the secret is Henry's unwillingness to become indebted to the Pope for this privilege in relation to Ireland. But then the simplest way to avoid getting a favour was, not to ask it ; and those who support the privilege say that he sent a solemn embassy to the Pope to ask it. What a strange mode of avoiding getting this same favour from the Pope. If there was a secret, the obvious and, so far as I know, the only tolerable explanation of it is, that Henry had the *Laudabiliter*, of his own manufacture, up his sleeve, ready to be launched or withheld as State policy might dictate when the parties to whom it was to be attributed were no more, and the danger of repudiation was over.

Explanation number two says the privilege was not worth mentioning. Not worth mentioning in a book on politics, though worth mentioning in a book on logic ! Not worth mentioning by the man who is said to have procured it, although he is a man addicted to gossiping about trifling incidents of his own life! And they who hold at one point of their argument that the privilege was not worth mentioning are the same people who tell us that John of Salisbury, three bishops, and an abbot were sent to the Pope specially to solicit this very thing which, when obtained, is not worth mentioning in an account of the mission written by one of the parties. If this is not an attempt to blow hot and cold out of the same mouth, I know not what is.

If either the chapter or the Bull is spurious, both are certainly so. As a spurious chapter could not have been circulated, except privately, without risk of repudiation while John of Salisbury lived, we get 1180 as the earliest date at which the chapter can have been made public, "It is not absent from a single copy of the *Metalogicus* and is, therefore, no interpolation," writes an ardent upholder of the supposed Bulls. Mark what a perfect statement we have here, clear, explicit, and uncomprising. What is its value? If correct it will bear examination. Let us see. The writer does not say that he has examined a single manuscript copy of the work. If you believe he has, as his statement induces you to do, you are convinced at once. If, in fact, he has not, which is extremely probable, his statement amounts to no more than that a printing machine has turned out a number of copies exactly alike, and you begin to suspect that he has been jesting or taking an advantage of you. The work was already old when printing became possible; the two or three editions of it that have been printed are nearly alike and may have been produced from the same manuscript copy, and all friends of the alleged Bulls are heartily welcome to any comfort they can derive from a resemblance due to the uniform action of a printing machine. A spurious chapter at the end of a work is by no means incredible to people acquainted with the liberties sometimes taken in the days of manuscript books; and I am confident that every reasonable reader will think he has now had ample proof that the chapter we are dealing with is spurious.

It will scarcely be asked what motive there was for writing this spurious chapter, for the motive has become obvious more than once in the course of the argument. The impulse to gratify such a man as Henry II. is a motive of dangerous power. He whose wish was so promptly obeyed in the murder of Thomas à Becket could have experienced no difficulty in getting a clever man willing to write a false chapter at the end of a book, and any Bulls or other documents his interest demanded. The work was not done perfectly, a forger's work rarely is. Yet it was not done without considerable skill. Each document might pass muster if not examined closely and checked with the other and with the facts of the time. Had they been genuine, this checking would have strengthened both. It has had the opposite effect. It has shown the documents to be antagonistic, irreconcilable, mutually destructive.

The limits of space forbid the development of all the difficulties that stand in the way of ascribing the last chapter in the *Metalogicus* to John of Salisbury. But the question remains: Why was it with his work that this liberty was taken? Although the answer may have been gleaned in the argument, it had better be formulated expressly. It is very simple. It is of the essence of forgery to seek a victim possessing the greatest number of points of probability and speciousness, and to make the false writing resemble his as closely as possible. The matter of the chapter being desirable to Henry, there was not a man in all his dominions to whom it could be more plausibly and effectively attributed than John of Salisbury. His career, his pliant character, and his mode of life eminently fitted the part. Well known as a man accustomed to write letters for other people, and, therefore, possessing facility in expressing thoughts other than his own, on an occasion arising for a State forgery, he stood marked as precisely the man whose work might be so tampered with most effectually. We have it on his own authority, in language amounting to a solemn oath and addressed to the King, that forgery was committed in his name. We have found that if the *Laudabiliter* is the letter to which the last chapter in the *Metalogicus* relates, the latter is false in its statements—false in the matters of which John of Salisbury had knowledge special and intimate, was written for a base purpose, was intended to affect unjustly a whole nation, and was, in several respects, such as John of Salisbury could not, without crime, have written. To maintain that he wrote it would be to maintain that he wrote for hire deliberate falsehoods of the greatest magnitude. This would be such a grave charge against John as we cannot accept the responsibility of making, in face of all the strong reasons already urged, and in face of the purity, grace, and plausibility of John's character, as revealed in his writings. The conclusion is that, by whomsoever written, the most venerable document adduced to prove the authenticity of the *Laudabiliter* is itself a spurious document, imparting discredit and not support. In destroying it we have necessarily damaged the *Laudabiliter*, of which it has always been the strongest prop. We, therefore, part company with John for the present, leaving, in our opinion, his character intact, his hands clean: but the chapter utterly destroyed, and the *Laudabiliter* deprived of its support and gravely damaged. On the latter, however, let judgment be reserved until we have completed our inquiry.

CHAPTER III.

Character of Giraldus Cambrensis.

THE reader is invited to maintain and fortify during the examination of the second witness for the Bulls that attitude of judicial impartiality found to be so necessary during the examination of the first. John of Salisbury, having nothing relevant to tell us, has been turned out of court. Giraldus Cambrensis is a bearer of evidence. He is the only original bearer of the two principal Bulls, and of doubt regarding the authenticity of one of them, and he says that both were published at a Synod of Bishops at Waterford in 1175. That is all the direct evidence he bears, and no one else bears any evidence. We have already partially examined the Bulls, and will complete the work in due course. The immediate question of supreme importance is, whether Giraldus is or is not a credible and irrefragable witness when he 'makes statements in themselves improbable, stands unsupported, and admits doubt to some extent. It is important, because on our decision with regard to it hinges the further question, whether we are to believe the Bulls to be genuine or not. "Among the good rules of honest history, that is certainly not the hindmost which directs a reader desirous of ascertaining the truth of what is narrated to give little heed to the number of writers, but a great deal to the trustworthiness of the first writer from whom others have copied."—White's *Apologia*, p. 194. To copy the Bulls from Giraldus is not to confirm him or them; and as this is what contemporary and subsequent writers have

E

done, they add no element of certainty, and he remains the sole support of those documents. Before him they were never known. Beyond him, or to any other besides him, the text of them has never been traced; though, to be genuine, that under Adrian's name should have been written more than thirty years before Giraldus wrote, and there were in the meantime writers in abundance and with ample facilities for copying. On him, therefore, and on him alone, they must depend. If he by himself is a really reliable and sufficient support, they stand. Were he to fail as a witness, they should be abandoned. This question cannot be considered without considering and testing his character, and especially his veracity. A clear conception of the entire man, his principles, motives, and methods, is essential to impartiality and justness of decision, and will at the same time greatly conduce to brevity in dealing with his statements and in the entire remainder of our discussion. Fortunately, a study of Giraldus himself will also be in accordance with his own ideas; for, be it innocence or be it vanity, he considered his character as admirable a subject as could occupy the mind of man, and the study of it was always gratifying to him. With us the result may be different.

His is a most difficult character to study or to delineate impartially. Himself a combination of antitheses and full of exaggeration, he generates exaggeration in his readers, being for some a hero, for others a monster. Anyone now reading an account of him for the first time will do well to start with the belief that he was neither. Many of my readers have already made acquaintance with him, and are competent to judge with what success I try to avoid both extremes.

Giraldus de Barri is best known as Cambrensis from his native country, Cambria or Wales:—

> "Kambria Giraldum genuit, sic Cambria mentem
> Erudiit, cineres cui lapis iste tegit."

He was the son of an Anglo-Norman father and of a Welsh mother, both of whom were of high rank and influentially connected. He was a nephew of David Fitz Girald, Bishop of St. David's, the most skilful and influential abettor of Dermot Mac Murrough and the man who did most to raise, chiefly from among his own kindred, the band of Welsh-Norman soldiers who first came over to recover Leinster for Dermot and for themselves. In his childhood Giraldus manifested so much talent and piety that his father was accustomed to call him "the little bishop." The desire thus early inculcated was doomed to disappointment, but not owing to deficiency of talent. Rather the contrary; for Giraldus was the most brilliant man Wales had till then produced, or produced for long after. He was, like John of Salisbury, a priest and a man of exceptional ability, but of a different type in both respects. His works are far better known than John's, and have always enjoyed a considerable amount of popularity. He was a more prolific writer, too, being a man of quicker wit, greater fluency, and writing with less regard for consistency and less deliberation. His Latin is occasionally corrupt, but it is very brisk, animated, and readable; and, no matter how trivial or commonplace his theme, interest in it never flags. He was a man of extensive reading and great versatility, but of an exaggerated sensibility, and so excitable and fanciful that he wrote, and perhaps believed for the moment as facts, absurdities that existed only in his own disordered brain or were gathered from no matter what quarter. With little fixity of conviction, except in the matter of his own greatness, he adopted statements and opinions on impulse, not on reasonable grounds; and even had he been more careful to reconcile them than he was, thus drawn from different extraneous sources and by an ever-changing process, his statements should necessarily be, as they are, frequently preposterous and in conflict with each other.

Endowed with some of the finest qualities, he had in him the spoiling, and more than the spoiling, of every one of them; so that as a literary man he can on the whole be regarded only with regret as self-spoiled. He knew not his merits from his defects, he had no regard for proportion or moderation and little for the discipline of truth. He makes some of his silliest statements with a solemnity so grave that it seems almost sincere; but sincere only for the moment, for on his next literary flower his hum may be different and even contradictory. Of true disinterested sincerity, of which self-sacrifice is the test and constancy the mark, he had none. He is most eloquent in invective, but he attains his highest level of merit when depicting in a scarcely conscious manner what he really knows. All his works are sprinkled with personal sketches of the appearance, character and habits of the leading men with whom he is dealing. These sketches are really excellent, piquant, animated and vivid. Although they all show bias, favourable or unfavourable, and in many instances conceal a treacherous dagger; yet, being clearly drawn from life, they must be in the main true, and they are of considerable literary and historical interest. The hearts for which the daggers were intended being long still, a reader may now enjoy the sketches without remorse. They form perhaps the most delightful part of all Giraldus's writings, and in their class have seldom been surpassed in any age. But he too soon becomes self-conscious, and wantonly spoils his best effects before they are completed, by reverting to his vice of counter-balancing antitheses which he wrongly believes to be his highest art. So infatuated is he with his literary theory that he adheres to it in defiance of truth and reason. If, outside his own immediate relatives, he finds himself obliged to give anyone credit for a good quality, he promptly adds credit for some very bad vice as a counterpoise. Both accounts may have been true of many of his subjects;

but where the fact failed in this respect he did not hesitate to invent, not in pure malice, but for the sake of his moral theory that great virtues were usually counter-balanced by great vices, and his corresponding literary theory that this mode of presenting the matter was the only one that gave the necessary variety and harmony to his story. Throughout all his works he is influenced by this theory even in his choice of words, and he delights to play upon and place in juxtaposition words nearly alike in sound but opposed in meaning. These cunning trifles lose their rhythm, their sole merit, in the process of translation from one language to another, and are indeed little better than puns. They are not the form which real power assumes in literature, nor are they worthy of such power as Giraldus possessed. They help the reader along by showing a pleasing agility in the manipulation of words, as goats among rocks enliven a landscape; but when overdone, as with Giraldus, the practice becomes a vulgar vice. By his weakness for scandal also, and by making his literary work the vehicle of his personal jealousies and animosities, Giraldus has revealed himself more truly than the things he meant to reveal; and while effectually excluding his works from the highest class, has imparted to them a vitalizing quality of a lower order which never fails to attract readers. After the readers have enjoyed him, few of them will close the book with that respect for Giraldus to which he expected his works would give him an indisputable title. They are more likely to dismiss him with that contemptuous charity which would have most galled him in life.

In England he has always been considered an interesting rather than an important author, and his popularity has always rested and still rests on the unfailing charm and freshness of his romance; for his writings are generally regarded as to a large extent romance irrespective of the nature of his ostensible subject. So far as they related to

England, Englishmen were able of themselves to discriminate between the grotesque exaggeration and the reality; and the writings were enjoyed for their own sake, the statements they embodied being rejected or mentally sifted. So far as the works related to Ireland, though they were at least as grotesque, some English writers have professed to believe them, just as some profess to believe caricatures of Irishmen to the present day—because they wish those things to be true of Irishmen, and would feel pained if disabused. Giraldus was the first to pander to this base appetite.

In Ireland so long as Gaelic literature prevailed few beyond the Pale knew Giraldus, and those few appear to have regarded him with contempt. After the destruction of Gaelic under Queen Elizabeth, the literature of England and of the Pale began to spread; and when the Irish became acquainted with Giraldus they took him more seriously than he had ever been taken before. The learning and literature of the country ceased to be Irish and gradually became Anglican. James Ussher, Peter Lombard and David Rothe were amongst the first distinguished men of the new era. Their learning being essentially that of England, and Gaelic having for them little more than an antiquarian interest, they sought no Irish corroboration, made no inquiry, evinced no doubt; and for the first time since they were written Giraldus's statements were accepted as those of a serious historian if not a sage. The Irishmen named repeat his statements on his authority, whatever that may be worth, naming Englishmen who have done the same, but neither producing nor seeking any other original authority. Their adhesion to the alleged Bulls therefore amounts to no more than that Giraldus had said so. That was known before as well as after. They do not add a pebble to the structure raised by him. We are thus thrown back upon him. Whatever be the quarter to which we address our

questions, echo answers—Giraldus. No one having so
far attacked or exposed Giraldus, and the cause in which
he wrote being in the ascendant and at the same time in
need of continued support, his reputation was rather a
thing to be sustained in the interest of established
authority. Unfortunately it was in the same interest that
the smaller of the two nations then in Ireland, in pursuit
of the policy and by the aid of an external power, denied
and penalized the acquisition of knowledge by the larger,
to the permanent injury of both, or rather to the injury
of the whole which the union of both should have constituted. In spite of the hard conditions and difficulties
which the Penal Laws threw in the way of literary effort
and historical research, two Irishmen of the seventeenth
century managed to throw some light upon Giraldus from
the effects of which he has never recovered. One was
Stephen White, S.J., author of the *Apologia pro Hibernia*;
the other was Dr. John Lynch, Archdeacon of Tuam,
author of *Cambrensis Eversus*. Subsequent research has
shown that some of their assumptions were incorrect; but
this is not so to a greater extent than is usual in English
historical works of the same century. Subject to these
corrections, their estimate of Giraldus is substantially that
which has since prevailed in Ireland, and which also
prevails in England, as we shall see. The *Cambrensis
Eversus* was honestly written with the means at the
author's disposal; and after all deductions have been made
it contains numberless shrewd and sound points brilliantly
expressed which still remain absolutely unshaken and
which are so many nails in Giraldus's coffin. In Ireland,
however, some have with less knowledge gone further and
painted Giraldus without a redeeming trait. This seems
to have occasioned in his favour a partial re-action which
happens to find expression in two works of peculiar and
permanent importance.

The *Apologia* is a small work and remains in its

original Latin. The *Cambrensis Eversus* is a great and elaborate work of historical interest extending far beyond the questions connected with Giraldus. It has been translated, and unfortunately edited also, for the Celtic Society by the Rev. Matthew Kelly of Maynooth College. The editing is unfortunate because it consists not in correcting typographical errors, for the work is full of them; not in supplying a correct index, for the one supplied is the most worthless specimen I know; not in helping the reader to gauge the true value of the work, for although the editor makes notes on almost every page of the three volumes, he does not devote a single one of them, not a word of his own from beginning to end, to appreciation of the author's work. It will be asked with incredulity what are the notes about. The crowded notes on page after page are, almost without exception, devoted to the graceless task of belittling and refuting Lynch and trying to restore Giraldus whom Lynch had upset. In the whole range of literature there is scarcely another work so unsympathetically edited, so gracelessly spoiled. The indefensible freak of entrusting the editing of this important work to a sullen opponent of its author and blind admirer of Giraldus greatly simplifies the question —What has become of the Celtic Society? The text and translation should be republished under the old name; but if the notes are worth publishing they should certainly stand in a separate volume suitably named as an attempted refutation of Lynch. Dr. Kelly expressly admits that he has made no special study of the subject, and that his "opinion rests mainly on the authority of Giraldus," supplemented by the dogmatic assertions of Mr. O'Callaghan. This latter authority he is obliged to reject when he comes to treat of matters of which he himself has made an independent study. In matters touching the liberty of his own nation he without study or inquiry accepts this authority, accepts the Bulls and apparently all the libels of the Middle Ages so far as they applied to Ireland, in opposition to the author he is translating, who had made a special study of the subject. I invite the reader to say is that an attitude of judicial impartiality worthy of the subject. Please bear the answer in mind while we proceed.

The *Macariæ Excidium* is a sketch of the Irish part of the war of the Revolution which drove James II. off, and placed William III. on, the throne. It was written by Colonel Charles O'Kelly who had taken part in that war as an officer in James's service. Being thus an account of the war at first hand, and the only one on the Jacobite side, it is a work of considerable value with reference to that particular war, but of none beyond that. It is said to have been originally written in French, but the only manuscripts of it known to exist are in Latin. Before entering on his proper subject, the writer presents, by way of introduction, and as conducive to a better understanding of his subject, a brief outline of Irish History from an early period down to the time of the war. As might be expected, such learning as is here displayed is superficial and is rather that of the Pale than Irish. The whole work is divided into short paragraphs numbered consecutively. In one of these it is stated that Pope Adrian, being an Englishman, had shown undue favour to the king of his native land by improperly granting him a Bull purporting to confer upon the king the dominion of Ireland—a thing he had no power to confer. Observe that this statement is founded not on the alleged Bull itself, inconclusive as that would be, but on the garbled traditional version of it fostered by English colonists and officials in Ireland. This work has been translated and edited for the Irish Archæological Society by Mr. J. C. O'Callaghan, and this paragraph is the peg upon which he hangs much learning on the subject now under consideration. His opinion, like that of Dr. Kelly, rests mainly on the authority of Giraldus, since for the two principal Bulls there is no other original authority. Taking Giraldus's dose without the salutary grain of salt gave him an appetite for more . He ransacked old pigeon-holes for libels and hobgoblin tales on any authority, or on none, succeeded in conjuring up a frightful picture of the irreligious and immoral condition of mediæval Ireland, and worked himself into such a state of mind that he believed it all; for what he has written on the subject is as if written under the influence of a nightmare. He never questions the credibility of Giraldus or of any other witness. So long as the story is sufficiently rank and strong he does not ask who bears it or whence it comes. Any bearer of it is credible enough for Mr. O'Callaghan, and with a few dogmatic sentences he affects to settle the matter while really contributing nothing to its elucidation. He gives no heed to the fact that not one of these five Bulls was known in Gaelic Ireland, where, if genuine, they should have been known, and where of course they would have been known, communication between Ireland and Rome having been all along frequent and constant. Having found the group of three Bulls which were not known in either England or Ireland until the eighteenth century, which were certainly never delivered to the persons to whom they were addressed, and which our friend Giraldus never heard of, nor any historian since, so smitten is Mr. O'Callaghan with them because of the foul charges contained in one of them, he actually quotes the three at full length twice over in his notes to this single volume, the subject of which is the Jacobite War! Again I ask the reader to say is this judicial impartiality, and to bear the answer in mind while we proceed.

The Very Rev. Dr. Malone says, with good-natured familiarity, " So much importance do I attach to Gerald Barry's statement, that I give up Irish authorities for him." And again, "Let us refer for a moment to Gerald Barry—no man was more competent to speak of the privilege. He was born about 1150; was tutor to Prince John; accompanied him to Ireland, and was subsequently bishop of St. David's. He published his *Conquest of Ireland*, containing the privilege, about the year 1188, and dedicated the latest edition of his work, in 1202, to his former pupil King John." And he goes on demonstrating in the most satisfactory manner what a splendid character and unimpeachable witness Giraldus is—a golden eagle not liable to lose a feather. He never gives his reader a hint that Giraldus was addicted to telling tales, or the prey of an extravagant imagination, or even a credulous listener. The importance of this magnificent encomium arises from the necessitous condition in which the Bulls are, depending on the evidence of this solitary witness. Since all other persons who mention the Bulls derive their text from this witness, the whole burden of proof rests upon him alone, and if his credibility were shaken all was lost. The Bulls and Giraldus's character for veracity must stand or fall together. Hence the necessity for the glowing testimonial.

One feels shy to bring abruptly into close proximity with such warm admiration and implicit faith a true account of the real Giraldus; for no matter how considerately stated the contrast is so violent as to seem almost rude. When a gentleman chivalrously declares his willingness to give up Irish authorities for Giraldus, it seems unkind to remind him that by doing so he would make no sacrifice whatever, there being no Irish authorities in this matter to be given up. But as such feelings of delicacy would paralyse inquiry and perpetuate error, I hope to be pardoned for taking the risk. The author of *Cambrensis Eversus*, an Irishman of unquestioned honour, honesty, and ability, having made an exhaustive study of Giraldus, is the proper authority for an Irishman to go to for a correct estimate of that gentleman. However, since Dr. Lynch's avowed purpose was to refute Giraldus, and since the matter here in question is one affecting Ireland, it will be more manifestly and abundantly fair to quote not from Lynch but from Englishmen of the very highest competence who stand like Giraldus on the side of the invaders, to quote—namely, from two of the editors of Giraldus's complete *Works* published by the authority and at the expense of the State. These gentlemen speak calmly, with the fullest possible knowledge, and with no rickety Bulls to uphold. A comparison of what they say will show at a glance if there is anything unfair in my description of Giraldus, and if we ought to "rely mainly upon Giraldus" and "give up Irish authorities for him." In the preface to Volume V. of the *Works*, the Rev. James Dimock says:—

"Giraldus was replete with the exact qualities, the very reverse of what are needed to form an impartial historian. A man of strong impetuous feelings and violent prejudices, with a marvellously elastic self-confidence that nothing could put down, an overflowing self-conceit that would be deemed a mere absurd caricature if any one but himself had depicted himself; he looked down with sublime contempt upon everyone and everything that did not agree with his own notions; he had not an idea that anything he thought or said could by any chance be wrong; he could not imagine any one who differed from him to be other than a fool or a rogue; ready as he was to find fault with any one except himself, yet sometimes an unflinching partizan, but often a virulent antagonist, he was the man of all others whose nature rendered it simply impossible for him to write a fair history of any sort, and least of all of Ireland, and the Irish, and the English invaders, with so many of his own near relatives amongst the latter. He was, too, one of those clever, ready-witted, ready-penned men, who are so apt to let their pens run away with them. He dashes away, often plainly on the impulse of the moment, and with him often a very impetuous impulse; and there is no argument sometimes in favour of what he is advancing too absurd for him, or too inconsistent with what he may have said a few pages before, or may have to say a few pages after; there is no assertion sometimes too bold, no invective against an opponent too virulently unjust, no imputation of the basest motives too manifestly unreasonable, and no assumption of the vilest and most horrible calumnies as certain truths too atrocious for him. Still he was a very fine fellow. The sin of unscrupulous assertion and invective was a sin of the age, and must not be laid exclusively upon him though, perhaps, by no writer more thoroughly given way to."

In the preface to Volume VII. of the *Works*, Mr. Freeman says:—

"In estimating the historical value of any work of Giraldus Cambrensis, we must remember the two-fold character of the man with whom we are dealing. We are dealing with one who was vain, garrulous, careless as to minute accuracy, even so far careless as to truth as to be, to say the least, ready to accept statements which told against an enemy without carefully weighing the evidence for them. We are dealing with one who was not very scrupulous as to consistency, and who felt no special shame of contradicting himself. But we are also dealing with one of the most learned men of a learned age, with one who, whatever we say as to the soundness of his judgment, came behind few in the sharpness of his wits—with one who looked with a keen, if not an impartial, eye on all the events and controversies of his time—with one, above all, who had mastered more languages than most men of his time, and who had looked at them with an approach to a scientific view which still fewer men of his time shared with him."

A duty sad and singular now devolves upon us. We must divest poor Giraldus of mitre, crozier, and episcopal purple, and deprive the Bulls of these supports so sorely needed, but, alas, fictitious. For those who knew Giraldus better than we do were so unkind that they never made him a bishop. This was really too bad, and shows a deplorable lack of consideration for people who undertake to sustain his Bulls; but it is rather late now to mend the matter. Giraldus never was Bishop of St. David's or of any other See. A mitre-hunter all his life, he never had the satisfaction of wearing one as a bishop. In his writings and in his conversation he commonly boasted that he had been offered and had rejected at different times at least half-a-dozen mitres, namely, those of Wexford, Leighlin, Ossory, Cashel, Bangor, and Llandaff. But he was of opinion that only a metropolitan one would fit him, and this or any other he never succeeded in obtaining. Possibly he would have been a better man as a bishop than he was as a priest, and according to his own account of the Church of England and Wales in his time, it would not have been difficult for him to excel as a bishop. However this may be, a bishop he never became; and, at one stroke, so much of his character goes by the board. The eagle begins to moult.

Giraldus may, without any injustice, be classed among the superfluous priests mentioned in the first chapter, who were not overpowered with any undue sense of the sacredness and responsibility attached to Holy Orders, but appear to have looked upon them as little more than a university degree or a qualification for some higher office in Church or State. He was far from being one of the worst of that class; and I think his faults and the faults of many of the class were not due to inherent badness of disposition. They had become priests in obedience not to any religious vocation but to the necessities of the meagre civilization of the time which offered to gentlemen few professions or modes of living at once civil and secular. Born into a world which contained no really appropriate sphere for them, they adopted the best available; and if they did not all adorn it, some of them did, and many of them were very far from being as vicious as their mental equipment would have enabled them to become. Had they been born to the fuller and more diversified civilization of modern times, they would probably never have become priests, but would have adopted congenial secular professions or callings in which they might have become famous or useful men. Under the restraint which the telegraph imposes, Giraldus might have become a distinguished journalist. In a world containing neither journals nor telegraph, he was sphereless and insufficiently restrained. As a priest, he occupied a false position, and he deserves considerable credit for having conformed to it as well as he did. He wanted to become a reformer, forsooth, but was incapable of the essential preliminary of reforming himself, or even of realising that he needed reforming. He scourged severely with tongue and pen contemporary churchmen whom he considered vicious; but it detracts somewhat from his merit when we find out that they were mostly men against whom he had a personal grudge. Can malice and religious zeal co-operate thus; and if so, which was the larger ingredient in Giraldus's motive? The reader can solve this little problem at leisure; it is beyond my reach. Giraldus also scourged severely the rivals of his relatives. In this case, the religious element must have been small. He wrote some things for the glory of God; but he wrote more, and his best work, for the glory of his relatives. The promoting of his own and their prosperity was the supreme object of his life, and for him men were good or bad according to their attitude on that great question. In pursuit of his object, he found no difficulty in being at the same moment a sort of Welsh patriot, a flatterer of Henry II. before the public, and in secret Henry's severest critic.

With all this I believe, and will ask the reader to believe, that Giraldus's detestation of immorality was true and natural, and that, *to a certain extent*, he would give the vicious no quarter. We must find out where his limits lay. Large numbers of clergymen from England and Wales flocked to Ireland in the wake of the invaders, ostensibly to bring back the bestial Irish to civilization and religion, but really to share the spoils of the country which was being ravaged. They were, for the most part, such men as Giraldus would have lashed mercilessly in England. Apparently without any ties of duty or responsibility in their own country, they seem to have been free to go where they pleased and to do what they pleased; and many of them brought mistresses with them or found mistresses in Dublin. They were a disgrace to the priestly calling, and gave the utmost scandal to the Irish, whom they professed to have come over to civilize. Here was a pretty nest of vipers. It is said that St. Laurence O'Toole, Archbishop of Dublin, refused to 140 of them permission to officiate in his diocese, refused to give them absolution, and bade them go as reserved cases to Rome to seek absolution. Whether they all went to Rome on this errand, or found a shorter way out of their difficulty, we know not. In either case there is little rashness in assuming that gentlemen of such calibre so treated had little love for Laurence or his Irish, and would have been only too glad to help their countrymen if they could do so by anything so easy as the writing of libels or spurious Bulls transferring Ireland with all it contained to their own worthy king. Some of their letters, still extant, breathe the most unscrupulous malevolence, and are full of the most atrocious calumnies against the Irish bishops, priests and laity. Little wonder, after the provocation Laurence had given them. They had not far to seek for moral enormities to attribute to other people. Nor should we forget that there are to the present day people—aye, sanctimonious people—who would write of the Irish now just as those men did then, in spite of the fact, a thousand times established, that in domestic morals the Irish are the purest people in Europe. The idea that those visitors were to lead the Irish people to "put on innocence of morals," and were to carry out the other great purposes enumerated in the *Laudabiliter* would have appeared to them the best joke of the invasion. Probably, none of them knew anything of that document, unless one who may have been concerned in its concoction. To Giraldus's credit be it said, those men had no love for him, knowing, as they did, that he was no sharer in their ribaldries, but would, in England and Wales, have heartily denounced them. But that was the limit of his consistency. In Ireland he and they were compatriots in the enemy's country. Accordingly, in Ireland he is silent about their vices, though these must have been greater than in England. He came to Ireland first in company with his brother Philip in 1183, that is, eleven years after King Henry's invasion. He came to Ireland again, in the suite of Prince John, towards the end of April, 1185, and remained in the country until the Easter of the following year. As a courtier on tour among his kindred who were then raiding and marauding over the country, he was quite full of their spirit, and eager to assist and glorify them in any way in his power. His scruples, if he had any, were silenced by the excitement of the game. These circumstances were not particularly favourable to the making of deep and close observations among the Irish, or to the formation of correct opinions regarding them. This defect was remedied in a truly characteristic manner. His friends introduced him to some Irish story-tellers, and these he appears to have taken seriously. The sequel will show how they, in their own fashion, made game of him; for, although a shrewd observer in some respects, his gullibility was really astounding. During this second trip he made notes of the tales told him and of the observations made; and on his return to England he wrote from these notes, from memory and from imagination; first the *Topographia*, and later the *Expugnatio*. In the latter work he records the death of St. Laurence O'Toole, in November, 1180, at Eu, in Normandy, where he was long detained, Giraldus says, because, when attending the Council of Lateran at Rome, he had shown himself zealous for his own nation, and was suspected by Henry of having

F

acted against the honour of his regal dignity. During Laurence's absence the gay English clergy must have had a pleasant time in Dublin; and, no doubt, they were well pleased with the exile and death of a prelate who had been so troublesome to them. Under their charge the people of Dublin must have made enormous strides towards perfection. So King Henry appears to have thought, for it was not until the September of the following year that he was kind enough to appoint to the Archbishopric of Dublin an Englishman named John Cumin, a clerk in his service, who was at that time a layman. Cumin went to Rome, where he was ordained priest and consecrated bishop in March, 1182. On coming back to England, so assured was he that his countrymen were duly civilizing the bestial Irish, although, presumably, he drew a revenue from Dublin, he did not trouble himself to visit that city until August, 1184, and then only in obedience to the King's command, and for a political purpose. At the time of Giraldus's second visit to Ireland, Archbishop Cumin was in Dublin. Early in 1186 at a convocation of the bishops and principal clergy of the province, the Abbot of Baltinglass preached a sermon, in which he strongly denounced the immorality of the clergy who had come over from England, and said that the Irish clergy, who had hitherto been pure, were contracting this corruption, because it was impossible to touch pitch without being soiled. This enraged the clergy so alluded to, all the more because the charge was true. They engaged Giraldus to become their spokesman; and three days later, duly primed and prompted, he returned the fire, preached at the Irish bishops and priests right, left and centre, poured upon their heads a boiling torrent of abuse, criticised and denounced them and the "many vices and enormities" to which he had been told they were addicted. He should admit, he said, the exemplary and pre-eminent chastity of the Irish priests, their rigorous and faithful observance of their religious duties, their strict abstinence, often fasting till dusk. "But as they devote the day to works of light, so they devote the night to works of darkness." Observe the antithetical compensation. Giraldus would on no account lose the chance of uttering that sentence whether true or false. It was true to his idea of literary perfection; and if the fact did not correspond, then the fact was wrong. *Voilà tout.* His charges against the priests are general and vague, except in the solitary matter of intemperance. He is less reserved in dealing with the bishops, of whom he has not a good word to say. Some of them had committed the unpardonable offence of thwarting his relatives. He admits that one of them, St. Laurence O'Toole, had striven to unite the Irish for the purpose of driving the invaders out of the country. His chance had come to revenge such conduct and oblige his countrymen. Accordingly he has the insolence to tell the bishops that they neglect every duty of their office, and allow the most horrible enormities to flourish unchecked under their very eyes. "The Irish are of all nations the most ignorant of the rudiments of Christianity; for they have never yet paid tithes nor firsts, nor contracted marriages." "A bestial nation, living like beasts;" hardly within the uttermost verge of civilization; habitual and incorrigible thieves; utterly unscrupulous perjurers; living normally in incest, adultery, and fornication. Not an instance does he give, not a shred of evidence does he adduce, but hurls his foul charges against the whole Irish nation indiscriminately, knowing perfectly well that the greatest moral deliquents were like himself, strangers, and that if honest Irishmen had their own property his friends would have had none. Again turning more especially upon the bishops, the dead as well as the living, he says—"There has never been one of them found to shed his blood for Christ's Church, which Christ has founded with His precious blood. Hence all the saints of the country are confessors and no martyrs; a thing difficult to find in any other Christian kingdom. Hence the extraordinary fact that among a cruel and bloodthirsty people the faith was founded and has always remained lukewarm, and there is no crown of martyrdom for the Church of Christ." His explanation of this extraordinary fact is, that there never was anyone in Ireland willing to shed his blood for the Church; "not even one." It is hard to know whether one should be amused, disgusted, or angry with a man who allows himself to talk in this manner. He says the bishops and clergy were indignant, "and many heads arose in the assembly in insult and protest." He seems to have thought that the Irish bishops, failing to get anybody to kill them, ought to have committed suicide. The people who did not kill their bishops were bloodthirsty. The man who said so would not have risked his smallest finger for all the bishops and people in Ireland. All this only shows us that even saints are not so wise before the event as after; for, of course, it is clear that if St. Patrick had known what was coming he would have waited to take lessons from this tourist on stilts.

At that convocation the bishops and clergy, under the presidency of an Englishman, Archbishop Cumin, adopted some twenty canons or resolutions. These relate almost exclusively to ecclesiastical matters, and so far from revealing moral enormities of the Irish, they amount to a refutation on the highest authority of the insults of Giraldus and a declaration that some of the strangers were bad men, and that the urgent need of the time was not to reform the Irish but to save them from contamination. One of the resolutions declares that the Irish clergy had always been eminent for their chastity, and that it would be disgraceful of the Archbishop were he to allow them to be corrupted by the contagion of strangers.—Ware's *History of the Bishops*, p. 317. It is clear that the voiceless laity must be allowed to share in this vindication. Few of them can have been aware of the slanders; they must have felt very indifferent to them; and were it otherwise they had no organization to defend their character. When charges jointly made against both orders are refuted by the order which is capable of reply, the order having no such capability must in justice be allowed to share in the vindication. And this is to say, in other words, that the charges were false.

On the absence of martyrs, Giraldus records in another place the retort of the Archbishop of Cashel, "a learned and discrete man," to a certain busybody who was pestering him about the moral depravity of the Irish people and their want of martyrs. The Archbishop humbly admitted that Ireland's martyrless condition was inexcusable, but pleaded that now, a race who knew how to make martyrs having come into the country, the Irish would probably soon learn the art.

On the evening of the day on which our author so scandalously overshot the mark, John, Archbishop of Dublin, dining with Felix, Bishop of Ossory, asked the latter what he thought of Giraldus's sermon. "He said many bad things very cleverly," answered the Bishop. "He called us drunkards. Certainly it was with difficulty I restrained myself from immediately flying at him, or, at the very least, retaliating sharply in words." Giraldus had a narrow escape on that occasion. To most people it will always be matter for regret that the pious Bishop Felix succeeded in restraining himself, and did not give Giraldus in the flesh what he so richly deserved. By doing so he might have rendered a distinct service to Giraldus by rousing his slumbering conscience, and, perhaps, to posterity also by killing in the shell Bulls and libels then a-hatching. His knowledge of Ireland's true condition was actual personal knowledge, and his interest in her was of the deepest, while Giraldus was merely a prejudiced or indifferent stranger, speaking from a brief and making a brilliant use of a *tu quoque* argument. Can anyone doubt what would have been the reply of the pious Felix if he had been asked to "rely mainly upon Giraldus," and to "give up Irish authorities for him"?

Giraldus was not a man to compose and recite a brilliant paper, and then destroy it merely because the charges it contained were in part false and in part absurd. The world was entitled to know what its greatest genuis had said on a critical occasion; and, instead of feeling shame or tendering an apology, he inserts a *précis* of his disgraceful sermon, with slight variations, in four of his works, in order that no reader of his shall miss it. The Bulls, which are our main object, he inserts in the *Liber de Principis Instructione*, Distinction 2, chapter 19; in the *Liber de Rebus a se Gestis*, Book 2, chapter 11; and in the *Expugnatio Hibernica*, Book, 2, chapter 5; and in each of these cases—observe—he gives the Bulls in immediate connection with the libellous matter supplied to him for his insolent philippic just described. The same matter he also repeats in the *Topographia Hibernica*. Although not one of Giraldus's works is edifying, even when his subject is religious, they are all interesting, and it would be easy and amusing to prove by quotations from them, one by one, that in not one of them was he fettered by the requirements of truth. In this way such a case of self-contradiction, falsehood, and absurdity might be made out on his own authority, as few other authors, ancient or modern, would yield. Having regard to the reader's patience, a brief examination of the works just named, will probably afford as much light as our purpose needs and as Giraldus's character will bear.

CHAPTER IV.

Works of Giraldus Cambrensis.

EDITORS and commentators alike, whatever their views of the so-called Bulls, agree in holding that Giraldus is the first authority for their existence and for their text, that before him no writer mentions them, and that all contemporary and subsequent writers derive their text from some one of his works, most of them from the *Expugnatio*. All the copies given by other writers are more or less imperfect and incomplete, as are also the copies in the *Expugnatio*. The fullest copies are those in the *Liber de Principis Instructione*, from which I have quoted them. Of this work Giraldus himself says (*Works*, Vol. I., page 423) that it was one of the earliest written by him, although not finished until late in life. Here then we stand nearest to, if not at, the source of these two Bulls. Beyond this work from which I have quoted them no man has ever traced them. The work is expressly designed as a moral and didactic treatise for the guidance of princes and prelates of all time, explaining the virtues and manners that best fit them, the vices that most misfit them, and how they should be trained for their intended stations. It is divided into three books, parts, or as the author calls them "Distinctions." As usual with Giraldus, he does not adhere to his declared purpose beyond the first Distinction. It consists of moral rules and reflections. Some are original, but most are drawn from Scripture and from a very wide range of secular authors. The remaining two Distinctions purport to illustrate the application of the abstract rules contained in the first, to Henry, his sons, and other princes and public personages of that time, with a result in most cases so unfavourable that it then appears as if a severe criticism of those princes had been the author's real design. In this way the work becomes to some extent a contemporary history, and it contains some historical facts not to be found elsewhere, interspersed with graphic personal sketches of the various princes. These sketches and the second and third Distinctions which contain them are so candid that it would not have been prudent for Giraldus to publish them until the more dangerous personages so dealt with were dead or disabled. For this reason he held them back for many years, and published the first Distinction by itself with the following note at the end of it:—

"But as for the two Distinctions following, which treat of the success and glory of a certain prince of our own time, and of the subsequent fall of the same prince into ignominy, these are not yet fully and finally written and polished, and it seemed advisable therefore that, while the tempest rages and gathers force, they should in the meantime remain in hiding, and keep themselves from the touch, sight, and hearing of all, that so, existing as though they existed not, they may await a safer and serener season for going out into public, until the clouds and mists be dispelled and a brighter and clearer sun illumine the face of heaven and the surface of the earth."

Throughout the second and third Distinctions "tyrant" is the usual term applied to Henry; and he is repeatedly and scornfully described as a man married to the divorced wife of the King of France, and notwithstanding this and the existence of offspring, still continuing to live a life of immorality notorious to all Europe, and so conducting himself that his wife and sons had been driven to revolt against him. One short extract will best convey Giraldus's secret opinion of Henry:—

"He was from the beginning to the very end an oppressor of the nobility: weighing right and wrong,

lawful and unlawful, according to his own interest; a
seller and delayer of justice; in speech changeable and
crafty; a ready breaker, not of his word only, but of his
pledged honour and of his oath; a public adulterer, an
ingrate towards God, and destitute of devotion; a hammer
of the Church, and a son born for destruction."

He describes an occasion on which Henry, in a fit of
ungovernable rage, set fire to the city of his birth, then
marched away till he came to a height, looked back upon
the smoking ruin which himself had wrought, rebuked
God for having deprived him of the city he loved, and
vowed that in revenge he would cheat God of his own soul.
Cardinal Vivianus, whom Henry had alternately fawned
upon and imprisoned, and who knew Henry well, says,
"never did I witness this man's equal in lying." A living
genuine historian says:—

"The tenor of Henry's life was totally at variance with
the religious zeal which he occasionally assumed to further
his political objects. Personally stained with the foulest
crimes, condemned by the Church, he had not only
threatened Pope Alexander to recognise the antipope, but
had even declared that he would turn Mussulman; and
having thus carried his point with the weak Pontiff,
boasted publicly that he held the Holy See in his purse."
—Gilbert's *History of the Viceroys*, page 26.

The interjected remark attributing weakness to Alexander
is probably no more than an *obiter dictum*, not to be taken
as a deliberate judgment, the author's immediate subject
being not Alexander's character but Henry's. Alexander's
many condemnations of Henry, and indeed all his letters,
exhibit vigilance, vigour, and independence; and on the
difficult subject of antipopes, in which Henry was by no
means faithful to him, he displayed for many years, in
opposition to a powerful Catholic Emperor, courage, firmness, charity, and consistency, which at length prevailed,
and which entitle him to the greatest respect. All credible
witnesses who knew Henry when living, and all who have

studied him in documents since, are in substantial agreement with Giraldus's description of him, especially in giving him unstinted credit for duplicity; and the facts of his life, as recorded in the cold pages of history, render any other view of him impossible. He was wholly unscrupulous, but able and ambitious, and, therefore, not wholly bad in practice. Statecraft sometimes induced him to do what virtue and moral motives induced better men to do. Ambition was his sole inspiration, policy his sole conscience, now impelling, now restraining him. And while Giraldus had his candid description locked up ready to launch as soon as Henry was dead, he was one of the most ardent postulants for favours at the hands of the living Henry, and accepted all the favours he succeeded in obtaining, regretting that they were not more. He had flattered Henry in the *Expugnatio* already published as "another Solomon," "a king fired with a great desire for the glory of God's Church, and of the Christian religion," "our Western Alexander," "truly king and conqueror, controlling his wrath with bravery, restraining his anger with modesty." In the same work, it is true, he credits Henry with an ample share of vices; but he does it with such modifications, and in such an atmosphere of greatness, that it involves no risk.

Whoever makes statements essentially contradictory of each other disentitles himself to be heard, especially if in each case he makes them, as Giraldus did, with the object of gaining personal advantage. "Frequently and copiously he flatters the living Henry, praises him as a king in every respect extraordinary in the world, and, as he says, most eminent in wisdom, piety, courage, justice, learning, love of peace, clemency towards all, never known to desire or encroach upon what belonged to another. Yet in many other works published by Giraldus after Henry's death he execrates the memory of that king and pursues him with a most virulent pen."—White's *Apologia*, p. 1.

The second Distinction, chapter 19, contains the two
Bulls as quoted by me, and a statement to the effect that
they had been formally published at a synod of bishops
held in Waterford in 1175. The second and third Distinctions contain accounts of many visions vouchsafed to
Henry, to Giraldus, and to others, and numerous quotations from the prophecies of Merlin Celidon, with examples
of their fulfilment.

The *Liber de Rebus a se Gestis* is a sort of autobiography.
The author tells so much about himself in all his works,
that this special book on that subject consists for the most
part of extracts from the others; or perhaps it is the block
of which passages in the others are chips. He kept a
draft of it written up like a diary, from youth onwards,
but did not reduce it to its present form until late in life.
Since he had already confided most of its contents to the
world in other works, there was little occasion for it,
except for the purpose of bringing the facts and fancies
of his life more closely together, and emphasizing his own
importance. The work is divided into three books, and
is sprinkled with anecdotes, visions, and the prophecies
of Merlin Celidon. Chapter XI. of Book 2 contains the
Bull *Laudabiliter* without comment. The immediately
succeeding chapters summarise the author's abusive sermon
in Dublin. Having acquired an extensive knowledge of
vice in his own country, he found the Irish a convenient
people to whom he might attribute the worst he knew,
and with regard to whom he might accept without question, and repeat without remorse, the most scandalous
tales. This consideration and his craving for a set-off to
their real virtues, would have been ample motive for
Giraldus without any special antipathy. But the Bishops
had supplied a further incentive in daring to throw any
obstacles in the way of his friends. The Irish people,
it is true, were far too submissive, and were on that account entitled to charity and not slander from him; but

this view overlooks the difficulty, rarely surmounted, of pardoning people whom your brothers and cousins are actually engaged in plundering, especially if you are of a poetic temperament and desire that posterity should sing the praises of the successful plunderers. *Nemo sibi esse judex vel suis jus dicere debet.* When writing of things he knows, Giraldus gives specific details. In no place would he more willingly give them than here. This fact, coupled with his omission to name any immoral Irishman, or to give any particulars which could have been tested even at the time he wrote, goes to show that he spoke either from fancy or from vague information which could not be subjected to examination, and leaves us entitled to infer that the Irish of that day were as true to the spirit, if not to the letter, of Christian ethics as their ancestors had been centuries before, and as their descendants are to-day.

The *Expugnatio Hibernica* is the best written of all Giraldus's works, and opens with seriousness and solemnity. It is the work which both Dr. Malone and Mr. Dimock had chiefly in mind when writing the contradictory opinions quoted in the third chapter. It seems to have been Giraldus's ambition to write a prose epic or historical novel based on the invasion and conquest of Ireland by the Anglo-Normans. This would have been a creditable ambition. But its execution was not possible to him. He stood too near the events, and had too close an interest in the actors on one side. His mind was too small and biassed to allow, even for the sake of poetic justice, that any Irishman could be a hero; and to make heroes of his own brothers and kindred, without any worthy opponent, was as impossible poetically as it was untrue historically. No struggle, no hero. He has no Irish hero, unless we are to consider Dermot, the traitor, as one. Had he a spark of the generous fire of poetry in him, he would have made a hero of O'Rourke, Prince of Breifny, and thereby given some verisimilitude to his praises of his own relatives. Instead of doing so he alleges, on the flimsiest grounds, that O'Rourke attempted to act treacherously towards Hugh de Laci at a colloquy on the Hill of Ward. The Four Masters say it was de Laci who attempted the treachery, and succeeded. Be that as it may, it was O'Rourke's head that was on that occasion severed from his body, taken to Dublin, and placed over the Castle gate. His compatriots having thus the material advantage and nothing more to fear from O'Rourke, Giraldus had a chance of doing justice to O'Rourke, whose character was worthy to adorn an epic. This was more than he could afford.

This is how he treats Dermot MacMurrough to whom he and his owed everything. He says that after a certain battle in Ossory a trophy of human heads was piled up in honour of Dermot; that Dermot turned them over one by one in excessive glee, and jumped up in the air three times with his hands clasped. Then recognising one of the heads as that of a man whom he had hated in life, he held it up by the ears and hair and tore off the nose and lips with his teeth. That was Giraldus's conception of an Irish hero. Needless to say, he did not derive this horrible story from any Irish source. Embittered against Dermot as the Irish chroniclers of the time were, and ready as they were to say the hardest things of him, they record nothing of this ghastly occurrence. It remained to be written by a camp-follower of the tribe to whom Dermot had betrayed his country, and is a good specimen of the traitor's reward. And, although Dermot was well known to be a bad man and the leader of a bad, immoral, and unjust cause, that did not prevent Giraldus's uncle, the Bishop of St. David's, from espousing that cause.

Imperfect as was Giraldus's conception of his task, he did not adhere to it beyond the first book. The remainder

consists of patches hurriedly sewn together, not a uniform
web. The whole result of his effort is a congeries of
brilliant fragments which might have formed part of a
fine work, but could never of themselves have formed a
symmetrical whole. The promised epic becomes a mere
one-sided political pamphlet, acquiring by its brilliant
extravagance the character of romance. He provides
Greek epithets for his soldiers—Stephanides, Morcardides,
Giraldides, etc.—just as Vigil does in the *Æneid*, and he
makes his heroes address their men and one another in
those terms. Their imaginary speeches occupy considerable space. Though his heroes are all on one side, they
do not receive even treatment. He draws a sharp distinction between his relatives and their rivals, and weighs
their respective merits in very different scales. In this
work he states repeatedly that King Henry regarded with
disfavour all the proceedings in Ireland before his own
arrival; and in the nineteenth chapter of the first book
he says that, early in 1170

"An edict was issued by the King of the English that
no ship should on any account sail with hostile intent to
Hibernia from any part of his dominions, and that every
man of those who had already gone there should either
return before the approaching Easter, or be disinherited
from their lands and made exiles from his kingdom for
ever."

Henry doubted the loyalty of the first irregular invaders,
but Giraldus should have told us, if he could, how this
conduct of Henry's can be reconciled with the soliciting
of Bulls and a burning desire to act upon them.

After describing Henry's proceedings in Ireland, to
which we shall presently return, Giraldus says that Henry
left Ireland in April, 1172, having spent only six months
in the country, and not having extended his sway over the
whole of it. News had come to him at the same moment
that his sons were conspiring or in open rebellion against

him, and that two Cardinals, Albertus and Theodinus, had come into Normandy, sent by Pope Alexander III., to hold an investigation regarding Henry's complicity in the murder of St. Thomas of Canterbury:—

"They were reputed to be just and good men, faithfully chosen for this special purpose, *but still Romans;* and unless the king hurried to them, his whole kingdom and all his territories might be placed under interdict."

Henry hurried off, and on his way slept one night at Cardiff, where he had a vision, Giraldus says. A spirit, in the garb of a Teutonic monk, stood before him, and called upon him to enforce a more strict observance of the Sabbath in his dominions, promising him in return rich reward. In the introduction to the second book we are told that Henry had many other visions and premonitions, more fully set forth in the *de Principis Instructione,* thus proving that the last-named work was already written. We are favoured with many visions of Giraldus's own, also those of his brothers, and informed that the Anglo-Norman soldiers saw a phantom army in Ossory—a thing of frequent occurrence in Ireland. The application and fulfilment of the prophecies of Merlin Celidon are carefully pointed out step by step, and we are told that John de Courci, in his campaign in Ulster, owed his success on one decisive occasion to the dissemination by him of a prophecy of St. Columbkille to the effect that he was to be the victor. This story is true, but Professor Eugene O'Curry has shown, in his *Manuscript Materials,* that the prophecy in question was *made* as well as disseminated by de Courci, or by Giraldus for him. Giraldus enumerates five grounds on which the King of England was entitled to the sovereignty of Ireland. In another work he enumerates a different set of grounds. That did not matter: a highway robber could state five grounds, perhaps ten, on which he was entitled to your purse. This work is also enriched with brief accounts of certain wonders more fully set forth in the *Topographia;* and that work is here defended against the attacks of critics. How? By the observation that it contains no tales more wonderful than those to be found in the Bible! Out of such materials a brilliant writer can make an entertaining book, but not history. When this is the nature of what he calls his serious and solemn work, it may be judged what a free pen he wielded when the restraint of seriousness was absent.

Apart from producing copies of the Bulls in the three works now noticed, the only important statement Giraldus makes about them is that they were formally published at a Synod of Bishops held in Waterford in 1175. Writers in the English interest at that time have a superfluity of "Synods of Bishops" in Ireland: and to those who accept their statements it appears to be of no importance that the Irish Bishops had no knowledge of some of the alleged Synods. To constitute one of their Synods of Bishops, it was sufficient for King Henry to send an Englishman as Bishop to the See of Waterford or of Dublin, and with him another Englishman, at once Bishop and politician, as inductor. Two being plural, there was nothing to prevent their holding a "Synod of Bishops" in their drawingroom. There was no occasion to invite the old-fashioned Bishops of Ireland to attend, especially as the proceedings were likely to be more harmonious without them. A document published at such a Synod might, so far as the Irish people were concerned, as well have been published in England or in Aquitaine, or might as well not have been published at all. Such a publication would be a manifest farce. In this way some of the later alleged Synods of Bishops must be accounted for; while some of the earlier are pure fiction, devoid of even this shadowy foundation.

Roger de Hovenden was a grave chronicler, whose

authority is accepted for many things for which there is
no other authority. He had the advantage over Giraldus
of having been in King Henry's service as secretary at
the time of the invasion of Ireland. Writing an account
of Henry's progress, immediately after landing in Ireland,
he says:—

"On the fifteenth of the Kalends of November, the
festival of St. Luke the Evangelist, himself and all his
army proceeded to Waterford, an episcopal city, and he
found there William Fitz Aldelin, his dapifer (provider
for his table), Robert Fitz Bernard, and others of his
household, whom he had sent before him from England.
And he delayed there during fifteen days. And there
came thither to him, by his order, the King of Cork, the
King of Limerick, the King of Ossory, the King of Meath,
Reginald of Waterford, and almost all the powerful men
of Hibernia, except the King of Connaught, who said that
he himself was, by right, King and Lord of the whole of
Hibernia. Furthermore, there came thither to the King
of England, all the Archbishops, Bishops, and Abbots
of the whole of Hibernia, and they accepted him as King
and Lord of Hibernia, swearing to him and to his heirs,
fealty and the right to rule over them for ever. Following
the example of the clergy, the aforesaid kings and princes
of Hibernia accepted in a similar manner Henry King
of England as King and Lord of Hibernia, and became
his men, and swore fealty to him and to his heirs against
all men."

He then sets out the names of the four Archbishops,
attempts to do the same for the twenty-eight bishops,
but breaks down, and repeats:—"All these, both Archbishops and Bishops, accepted King Henry of England
and his heirs, as Kings and Lords of Hibernia for ever,
an act which they confirmed by surrendering their
charters to him." It would be difficult to find a statement
more explicit and convincing than this of a grave writer,
who was in a position to know the facts. What is there to
be said on it? So little foundation is there for saying
that all the Archbishops, Bishops, and Abbots of Ireland

visited Waterford, separately or collectively, in November,
1171, that those most willing to sustain the statement,
if possible, simply abandon it as substantially untrue,
and do not wish to be questioned about Roger de Hovenden
or his assembly of Bishops. Henry had landed at the
head of a magnificent army of Continental veterans,
armed and armoured in a manner never before seen in
Ireland. The leaders of the irregular invaders and the
Irish princes within his reach, understanding at once
that he was not to be trifled with, and not being madmen,
came and submitted to him. Some few Bishops and
Abbots of the adjacent districts acted similarly in their
individual capacity, without power or pretence to bind
anyone but themselves. The princes of Ulster and other
distant parts of the country made no move either to sustain
Roderick O'Connor, or to acknowledge Henry Plantagenet.
No Archbishop, Bishop or Abbot, beyond Henry's immediate reach, waited upon Henry at Waterford, nor did all
within his reach. Those who did wait upon him had no
charters to surrender. All this is now common ground
no longer in dispute, and the elaborate statement, based
on such frail material, is tacitly abandoned as substantially
untrue. We are, therefore, not called upon to prove its
untruth afresh, especially as it is not alleged that the
Bulls were published on that occasion. But we are entitled
to ask for what purpose was it written? For what purpose
did Roger specifically name, or try to name, thirty-two
prelates, representing every district from end to end of
Ireland, and say, and repeat, that all these came to Waterford and swore allegiance to Henry, the fact being, that
most of them never saw Henry in their lives, and never
tried to see him? The question does not admit of discussion. The purpose of the statement, whether original or
hearsay, was to help the cause of the invaders, and to
help it at the expense of truth. And if a grave and
responsible writer felt at liberty for that purpose to body

forth from shadow and imagination one complete assembly
of Bishops, how was an imaginative and confessed dreamer
to distinguish himself if not by recording three or four
Synods? Accordingly, Giraldus has (1) a "Synod of
Bishops" in Armagh in 1170; (2) a "Council of Bishops"
in Cashel in 1172; (3) a "Synod of Bishops" in Waterford
in 1175; and (4) a "Synod of Bishops" in Dublin in
1177.

(1) He is vague as to the date of this, and gives no
particulars of who were present or who presided. In
Labbé's *Collection of Sacred Councils*, Giraldus's vague
statement is copied verbatim without a word in addition,
but with this very curious heading: "SYNOD OF WATER-
FORD, held in Hibernia, about the year of Our Lord, 1158;
from the *Expugnatio Hibernica* of Giraldus Cambrensis,
chapter 18." Giraldus is, therefore, the sole authority for
it. His text places it among the events of 1170, and at
Armagh. A vague Synod on his sole authority, and un-
fixed in time and place, does not call for further
consideration.

(2) The Synod of Cashel is the only one with regard to
which Giraldus states by whom it was called, who attended,
who presided, and sets forth the resolutions arrived at.
The contrast will be best shown by an outline of his statements, although some of them cannot be accepted,
especially the first. He says that early in 1172, the
island having been reduced to silence by the presence of
King Henry, "the King, fired with a great desire for the
glory of God's Church and of the Christian religion,"
summoned a Council at Cashel, that this Council was
presided over by the Pope's Legate Christian [=Criostan
O'Conarchy], Bishop of Lismore, and that the following
Archbishops with their suffragan bishops and certain
other ecclesiastics of their provinces were present:—
Donatus [=Domnall O'Huallachain], Archbishop of
Cashel; Laurencius [=Lorcan O'Toole], Archbishop of

Dublin; Catholicus [=Chadhla O'Duffy], Archbishop of Tuam. There were also present on behalf of Henry, Radulfus, or Ralph, Abbot of Buildwas; Radulfus, Archdeacon of Llandaff; Nicholas, one of Henry's chaplains; and some other clergymen. He then devotes an entire chapter to the constitutions or decrees agreed to by the council. each of which he explains at some length. They fall under the following heads:—(*a*) marriages; (*b*) baptisms; (*c*) tithes; (*d*) immunity of church property from tax and every secular exaction; (*e*) immunity of the clergy from eric and other fines; (*f*) the making of wills; (*g*) funeral services; and also, he says, some decrees aimed at bringing the Irish Church into conformity with the Anglican in matters of discipline.

On his account of this Synod we have to observe, first, the absence of Gelasius [=Gilla-Isa Mac Laig], Archbishop of Armagh. Henry and his friends felt this; it is evidently a sore point with Giraldus, and he proceeds to take out satisfaction after his manner by raising a laugh at the Primate—

"The Primate of Armagh was not present then on account of feebleness of body and great age; but he afterwards came to Dublin and placed his approval of all things at the King's disposition. By common repute a holy man, he brought about with him wherever he went a white cow, whose milk alone he used."

The Primate was old, but not so feeble as is here represented. In 1171 he made an extended visitation of Ulster, and in 1172 he presided as Primate over an assembly of the Connaught clergy. A man able to do this could have easily gone to Cashel if so disposed. If he went to Dublin, it was an act of courtesy: for Henry had acquired no control over him or his district. Secondly, we have to observe the fulness and explicitness of the account as compared with the few vague sentences in which he disposes of the other alleged Synods. If on one side of this contrast his details are to be taken as proof that he had before him an official record of the acts of the Synod, it must follow with equal force that in the other cases he had no such record, and gives us nothing better than the rumours of interested persons. To maintain that details indicate genuineness is to admit that their absence indicates spuriousness. Thirdly, although his information with regard to the Cashel Synod must have been derived from minutes of the proceedings or a report drawn up for King Henry by the Englishmen present at the Synod, there are no shocking moral enormities revealed nor anything worse than what well might have to be considered by a Synod in any country in Europe in any age. Lastly, the report contains not a word about the *Laudabiliter*, nor does Giraldus mention it in connection with this Synod.

According to the foregoing indications, that of Cashel is the only genuine Synod Giraldus records. It was held while Henry was present in Ireland. That it was a most appropriate occasion for publishing a Bull on his behalf is self-evident. So favourable to him is the *Laudabiliter*, and so manifestly useful would its publication at that Synod have been to him, one would almost expect him to insist upon its publication there even if it were spurious; while, if genuine, the urgent moral need of the Irish, Henry's burning zeal for their conversion and for the glory of God and of the Church, and the warm approval of the Pope, would have made the publication of the *Laudabiliter* on that occasion a duty incumbent on Henry and on the ecclesiastics who represented him. It was not mentioned at all. The Pope's Legate was in the chair. Had the *Laudabiliter* been genuine he would have been made aware of its existence long before, and the formal publication of it while Henry was present in the country would have formed part, and, from Henry's point of view, the most important part, of the proceedings. But if that document was spurious, or not yet "written and polished," the Legate necessarily knew nothing of it; and it was more prudent for Henry to leave him so than to court exposure. It would be childish to urge that Henry had a genuine Bull and forgot it; but supposing that silly plea were tenable, the ecclesiastics present on his behalf might be trusted not to forget a matter in their own department and of capital importance to him and them. To remember his interest in this respect was precisely their business there. How could they remember a State Paper which perhaps they had never seen? Ah! the gentlemen who ask this question forget their own arguments. They are the same who tells us that the *Laudabiliter* had been read in England, sixteen years before, at an assembly of notables. They are the same who tell us that an assertion of its existence had been for thirteen years before the world in the *Metalogicus* which these ecclesiastics must be taken to have read. On which side stands the difficulty now? My contention is that the reading before the notables is mythical, that the statement now at the end of the *Metalogicus* was placed there subsequently by a strange hand, and that the *Laudabiliter* was not read at Cashel for the simple reason that nobody at that Synod knew it existed. No one has ever claimed that it was read there; and Giraldus's statement in the next paragraph is tantamount to an assertion that it was not.

(3) We have proof that Henry and his representatives at Cashel were fully conscious of the value such an instrument as the *Laudabiliter* would be to them, and, therefore, that it was not through forgetfulness, but by design it was neither read nor mentioned at Cashel. In Chapter 5 of Book 2, Giraldus says that Henry sent messengers to Pope Alexander III. with letters drawn up at the Synod of Cashel, and took advantage of the opportunity

to ask the Pope's approval and authority for subduing the Irish people, and bringing the Church in Ireland under the same rules and discipline as the Anglican Church. He does not say who the messengers were or what was the nature of the letters they bore. He then proceeds:—

"The privilege was accordingly sent into Ireland per Nicholas, then Prior of Wallingford, afterwards for a time Abbot of Malmesbury, and William Fitz Aldelin; and a Synod of Bishops having been immediately called at Waterford, the same privilege was solemnly read in the public hearing with universal approval. Also another privilege sent per the same persons, which the same king had obtained from Alexander's predecessor, Pope Adrian, through John of Salisbury, afterwards Bishop of Chartres, who had been sent to *Rome* for that special purpose. Through whom also the same Pope presented to the King of the English a gold ring in sign of investiture; and this ring was immediately, together with the privilege, placed in the archives of Winchester."

He does not specify the date of this Synod, but makes the statement in the part of his narrative dealing with 1175. There is no mention of any Synod at this date in *Labbé*, *Wilkins*, or *Migne*. Cardinal Moran says that he has been unable to discover a particle of evidence that any Synod or Council whatsoever was held in Waterford in 1175, and that it is a myth. No evidence having since been produced, beyond what he had before him, we may conclude that there is none. No one in Ireland at the time knew anything of the alleged Synod. It remained for Giraldus to come ten years later and discover that it had been held. Had there been genuine documents to publish at an Irish Synod on Henry's behalf, he would have taken care to have them published at as large and representative an assembly as he could gather, so that all men might know; and the Pope's representative, then in Ireland, would have been connected with the proceedings, or at least aware of them. Had a Synod of that character been held, and made the occasion of an important proclamation, there would be no need to grope for it; the event would be writ large, and some authoritative record of it would remain for reference. There has never been a record of it, nor a reference by the English in Ireland to it, or to such a record. It seems to be another of those cases in which admirers of these Bulls claim publicity and secrecy at the same time. This is the only publication claimed for either of the two Bulls; though to be genuine, the *Laudabiliter* should have been written twenty years before. During all that time the Pope had a representative in Ireland who knew nothing about that document; and now it is published without him at a Synod of Bishops, not one of whom is named, and not a trace of whose proceedings remains. What is classed as the principal privilege is that of Alexander, and it is so classed by the author, who says that it was thought by some to be spurious. There is a certain appropriateness in assigning to a spurious Synod, the promulgation of spurious documents.

(4) Among Giraldus's records, under 1177, is this entry:—

"Meanwhile Vivianus, performing the function of Legate through Hibernia, called a Synod of Bishops in Dublin, publicly proclaimed *viva voce* the sovereignity of the King of the English in Hibernia, and its confirmation by the Supreme Pontiff; strictly directing and enjoining upon both the clergy and the laity, under threat of anathema, not to presume with daring rashness to withdraw in any respect from their fealty to him."

The holding of this Synod is briefly acknowledged by the *Four Masters*. There is nothing about it in Labbé's *Collection*, but Wilkins includes it in his *Councils of Great Britain and Ireland*, merely copying Giraldus's statement, and adding a note from Hovenden, not confirming that statement, but saying that Henry had arrested Cardinal Vivian when passing through England for having come into his dominions without asking his permission, and only let him go on his swearing that he would do nothing opposed to Henry's interests. If the alleged Synod was really held, we may observe with regard to it, that Giraldus says nothing about the Bulls having been read or mentioned on that occasion, though the purpose he attributes to Cardinal Vivian is the same as that which the Bulls profess. In Haverty's history it is stated, on the authority of the passage just quoted, that Cardinal Vivian insisted on the obligation of observing those Bulls. Father Morris maintains that the passage does not bear that interpretation, and that Cardinal Vivian knew nothing whatever about the alleged Bulls. Mr. Haverty proceeds to say of Vivian—

"He was probably induced by the English functionaries to take this step, as it does not appear that he had any commission from the Pope to do so."

That is to say, if Vivian did take any such action, it was political action, taken on his own personal initiation, and in what he considered the interests of peace and order. On this, I am of opinion—(1) That Vivian took no such action, because he knew that much the larger part of Ireland had not yet submitted to the invaders, and was in no mood to do so, and to threaten with his own anathemas the clergy and laity of that larger part for attempting a thing he knew they were absolutely determined to continue doing would be ridiculous. (2) Had the Bulls been genuine, Cardinal Vivian, coming to the country *a latere*, would have been in full possession of them, would have come to proclaim them with greater force than that of his own voice, and would not have been arrested by Henry on the way. (3) Had he done this, Giraldus would have been delighted to state expressly a fact so agreeable to him. This Giraldus has not done.

Before finally dismissing the *Expugnatio*, we may as well observe one or two more of the many instances in which Giraldus entangles himself, and all who believe him, in a snare of his own contriving. He says that Henry and the invaders were animated by a disinterested desire to reform the Irish and collect Peter's Pence for the Pope. Henry while in Ireland, and after going away, distributed amongst his favourites charters of lands in Ireland then in the undisputed possession of their Irish owners. These charters were practically licences to the donees to attack the owners of those lands by force and fraud *ad libitum* and thus to acquire the lands if they could. Force and fraud were practised, in some cases successfully, in other cases unsuccessfully. This was what the invaders meant by reforming the Irish—reforming them out of their property. And Giraldus in substance asks us to believe that this policy of pillage and plunder was carried on in pursuance of an inspiration from God and authority from the Pope, and that the Pope was to share in the booty. They are pretty documents for the proof of which this blasphemous theory is essential. It is, I need scarcely say, an absolute historical certainty that the Pope never received a penny from the Irish through the invaders.

Again, Giraldus says that St. Laurence O'Toole strove to unite the Irish for the purpose of expelling the invaders, and that Henry regarded Laurence with distrust and had him detained an exile in Normandy until he died there. If Laurence was then opposed to the presence of the invaders, as he undoubtedly was, is it credible, as required by the Bull theory, that he signed at the Synod of Cashel a petition asserting that those same invaders were bringing back the Irish to the ways of virtue, and praying the Pope to confirm their presence in the country? And if anyone is able to believe that Laurence acted thus falsely and treacherously towards his country *in the interest of Henry*, what reason remained for Henry to persecute Laurence as he continued to do until his death? These are difficulties of a class that arise only in connection with untruth. No explanation of them has ever been so much as attempted. None is possible, save that one which alone adequately explains these and all other difficulties, namely, —the alleged Bulls are spurious.

Let us now look into the *Topograj hia Hibernica*, which in the matter of marvels was to rival the Bible. It is a fantastic description of Ireland and the Irish, in which Giraldus has the frankness to admit that *in his writings relating to Ireland he derives very little assistance from Irish sources*. Of all his extraordinary statements, that is, perhaps, the one containing the greatest amount of truth. He tells some things that are true, some that are silly to tell whether true or false, some that no one would like to translate into English at the present day, some marvellous fancies and some deliberate falsehoods. From such raw fibre a gaudy web may be spun, and Giraldus is as facile a spinner of yarns and weaver of webs as need be wished for. It was not his intention to write light literature. He has done it unconsciously. He set about each of his works with much solemnity, yet, somehow, when finished, it was found to be light enough, and his solemnity only heightened the effect. His descriptions of some of the wild birds, animals, and fishes of Ireland are correct, and he notices the absence of the snake and the mole, which are common in England. But truth was altogether too tame for him. There were in Ireland biformed birds, having one foot armed with rapacious talons, and the other foot webbed for swimming. Then follow some indecent stable-yard jests regarding the origin of these and other monstrosities. Some storks in Ireland spent the winter at the bottom of rivers, under water of course, and came up alive and well in springtime. Weasels were able to restore their dead young to life. The genera-

tion and evolution of the birds called barnacles are
minutely described. At first slime of the sea, they afterwards became shellfish, and finally birds:—

"I have frequently seen with my own eyes more than
a thousand tiny bodies of these birds, enclosed in their
shells, and not yet fully developed, hanging from one
log of wood on the sea beach."

Nor are these things very wonderful, since there are, it
is said, grass-hoppers in Sicily which sing more sweetly
after their heads have been cut off than when whole, and
better dead than alive. Then our author becomes, or
affects to become, serious, and says that henceforth he will
insert nothing but what he has seen with his own eyes or
has been assured of on the most authentic human testi-
mony. After this undertaking one of the first things he
tells is that there is a lake in Munster in which there are
two islands. On the larger of these islands no creature
of the female sex can exist; it would immediately die on
entering. On the smaller island no person can die; hence
it is called the Island of the Living. "There is a well
in Munster, and anyone who washes in its waters immediately becomes gray." "There is, on the other hand,
a well in distant Ulster, and whoever washes in its waters
never becomes gray. Ladies frequent this, as do also men
who wish to avoid grayness." "A certain willow-tree,
not far from St. Kevin's Church at Glendalough, bears
apples." The ravens in the same neighbourhood kept a
fast-day.

"St. Kevin, praying in his cell one day, stretched forth
his hand through the window to heaven, in his accustomed
manner, and a blackbird came and laid eggs in the palm
of his hand, as in a nest. So patient was the Saint, and
so full of kindness, that he neither closed nor withdrew
his hand, but unweariedly kept it extended and open
till the young birds were fully fledged."

He gives a vague and mutilated outline of the fabled magical origin of Lough Neagh, and says that the fishermen see round towers beneath its waters. The wife of the King of Limerick had a beard and a mane. That must have been very becoming; but Connaught had something more exquisite still. A lady there had a shaggy beard on one side of her face, while the other side was quite hairless and womanly. The thought of this is enough to make the new woman die of envy. In one part of Ireland there was a half-man ox, having ox eyes and no speech, but lowing like an ox. In another district, in order to preserve the author's usual balance, there was a half-ox man. He has heard "from some sailors" who had been driven ashore by a storm on the Connaught Sea that they had met with Irishmen stark naked, excepting a belt of raw hide tied about the middle—men who had never before seen civilized people, a ship, bread, or cheese; had never used any clothes except their long hair, which hung plentifully over their backs; who asked for meat to eat, though it was Lent, because they had never heard of Lent, and did not know what it meant; did not know the year, the month, or anything of that nature; were completely ignorant of the days of the week; when asked if they were Christians or had been baptized, answered that they had never heard or known anything about Christ; and went away, taking with them a loaf and a piece of cheese, to show to their own people the sort of food foreigners ate. "Some sailors" were clearly the proper authorities for that yarn. "Still," he says, "it is extraordinary what a number of saints they have, and how devoutly they venerate them." It would be more than extraordinary if, at the same time, they had never heard of Christ. He tells wonderful things about certain mills, as that of St. Feichin at Fore; and says that some of those mills would not grind corn on Sundays. It was certainly a strange country where the mills remained so pious, while the people, though devoutly venerating their numerous saints, had lost even the recollection of Christianity. They had lost their clothes as well; but that was such a trifling detail that, in their comfort, they soon forgot they had ever worn any. They were obviously in need of Bulls to make them all right. After repeating the substance of his scandalous sermon in Dublin, he gives an outline of the history of Ireland from the earliest times to his own. It is based on the legends of the story-tellers, hammered into what Giraldus considers correct form; and our only regret is that he did not add a history of the future, both would be so appropriate in this work. Until times comparatively recent, Englishmen, unwilling to know the truth about a country so near them, professed to believe that this caricature was the true and only history of Ireland before the Conquest. In it Giraldus alleges four grounds of justification for the invasion of Ireland by Henry II., namely (1) that the kings of Ireland had paid tribute to the British King Arthur; (2) that the Irish had voluntarily submitted to Henry; (3) the Papal privilege; (4) the uncivilized and bestial condition of the Irish, some of whom had tails like animals, while those of normal shape had the manners of animals. The only art he credits them with is music; in which, he says, "they surpass every nation I have ever seen." He next introduces us to fleas in Connaught; but I beg pardon for having strained the reader's patience so severely.

We have now before us ample evidence on which to form an independent opinion on the question, whether the ingenious author of the works just glanced at is or is not a credible witness when he makes statements in themselves improbable, stands unsupported, and admits doubt to some extent. Hold up the balance, and let not so much as a breath of air affect its tendency. What we have been seeking in Giraldus, what must be found in him if the Bulls are to stand, is veracity. Have we found

that this is the quality for which he was distinguished?
Is he or is he not a true witness in whom, unsupported,
we can confidently repose implicit trust? Has he kept
in all his works the promise given in various words in
all of them to tell us the truth? Was he painstaking in
examining statements before adopting them, obedient to
the rein of conscience, grave and slow in undertaking
responsibility? Does not every reader who enjoys him
know that his special charm consists in his lack and
disregard of those qualities, and in his obedience to
passion and impulse? Do we, in other matters,
in any matter, accept the unsupported statements
of such a man? If we are prepared to accept
his unsupported statements, how many of them,
which of them? and on what principle are we to make
a selection? If he describes a hare or a badger, we know
how far he is right. If he makes historical statements
which are made by anyone else independently, or which
agree with the texture of history, we are satisfied. But
his visions, his vilifications of a people whom his
immediate relatives are engaged in fighting, his documents
which are part and parcel of the plot, these one and all
we reject with scorn; and we should not be sane people
to do otherwise. Sleek patrons manifest their peculiar
kindness to us by offering the compromise of cutting off
the tails he puts on our men, and the manes he puts on
our women, and letting the residue stand as correct.
Giraldus's gross statements are less offensive than such
a compromise. We will have none of it. We will allow
no pruning and tailcutting to be practised upon our
ancestors. If they must be credited with bestial manners
on the authority of Giraldus, they must by all means,
on the same distinguished authority, be allowed to retain
their then appropriate appendages of manes and tails,
horns and hoofs.

Sir James Ware includes in his work called *The Writers*

of Ireland, a notice of the *Cambrensis Eversus*, and on page 163, says of Archdeacon Lynch, the author of that work—

"He published this book under the feigned name of Gratianus Lucius, and compiled it in defence of his country against the fabulous and malicious reports made of it by Girald Barry, commonly called Cambrensis, wherein with a judicious and sharp pen he exposeth the numberless mistakes, falsehoods, and calumnies of that writer, showing, in confuting him, that he was well qualified to undertake the subject by a great compass of knowledge in the history of his country and in other polite learning."

The question of the authenticity of the Bulls is now nearly settled. To that end all that remains for you to do is to forget all Giraldus's fibs on every other subject on which he wrote, and believe all he tells you about Ireland. Let your "opinion rest mainly upon Giraldus." "Give up Irish authorities for him." Close your eyes to the fact that while he put tails on Irishmen, he forgot to put either heads or tails on his Bulls. He saw the Bulls with his own eyes—after he had written them. He presents them to you on the highest human authority—his own. If you are not satisfied, his works contain plenty of bad language, applicable to your unreasonable condition. If we were to treat him as a serious historian and credible witness, we should surely be bound to look to him for answers to some, at least of the important questions inseparable from that *rôle*. He being the only original bearer of the two principal Bulls is the person who should tell us most about them, is he not? Does he account for the absence of Henry's name from the beginning, the absence of Adrian's from the end, the absence of the Papal Chancellor's name, the absence of place of issue, the absence of date, or all or any of the discrepancies we have discussed? No. Does he fortify them by reference to any facts upon which we can confidently rely? No; on the contrary, he, the first bearer of these two consecutive instruments in a single transaction, one of them confirming the other, says that one of them is thought by some to be spurious, while he apparently derives both from the same source. This statement of his renders it *certain* that that one at any rate was not copied from a Papal original, and *highly probable* that the other was not either. Where did he find them? Was it in the same storehouse in which he found tails for Irishmen? Of course, he does not tell us. Where he found them is probably the last thing he would tell. He may have found them pinned to the brief on which he based his sermon in Dublin. You are offered Bulls, tails, horns, and all on precisely the same authority, and must judge whether that is sufficient to sustain all or any of them. If people who accept the Bulls are satisfied with their only indispensable witness, it seems to me that people who reject them have far more reason to be so. He was one of those dangerous men who write libels with a solemn face, and, while they themselves are the real criminals, presume to sit in judgment upon decent people. At the same time, without feeling any certainty on the point, I should ultimately prefer to believe that Giraldus was not the actual author of the Bulls, but was the dupe of some one more cunning. This opinion rests chiefly on the fact that he retained till the day of his death many of the ways of an overgrown schoolboy. He resembled one of those receptacles in public gardens into which people are invited to throw papers for which they have no other use.

The curious works we have noticed are in part true, in part consciously but innocently fictitious, in part unconsciously fictitious and due to the author's temperament and circumstances, and in part deliberately and maliciously false. The blending of these ingredients by Giraldus renders the net truth for ever inextricable. His materials and methods, suitable to a certain extent for poetry, are indefensible when he presumes or pretends to write history. The most lenient view of his work cannot exculpate him from having sacrilegiously polluted the fountain of Irish history for readers in England. On him must rest responsibility to a very considerable extent for the misunderstandings that have always existed between the two countries. Such conscience as he had was of the most flimsy and accommodating order. But he had some sort of conscience; for when the shadow of death began to creep over him, when, as he says, he had become an old man and desired reconciliation with God and the edification of posterity, he wrote a new introduction to the last edition of the *Expugnatio* prepared by himself. This will be found in Volume V. of his *Works*, and pages 409 and 410 are very touching. Looking back upon events in Ireland which, in the days of hot blood and effervescent brain, he had vainly dreamt of immortalising as surpassingly glorious, he is forced to acknowledge that the progress then hoped for has proved to be real retrogression, and he almost regrets the invasion and its deplorable consequences:—

"The evil plight of everything has become worse, because to the Church of Christ, newly come into our power, we have brought nothing new. Not only have we not judged her worthy of princely liberality and due honour, but we have even taken away her lands and possessions, and have systematically striven to mutilate or abrogate her pristine dignities and ancient privileges."

What a change this is from his insolent sermon in Dublin! Can anyone doubt as to which document contains the truth? Referring to the *Laudabiliter*, he says that the commission to exalt the Church has been turned into a commission to plunder churches: "Et sic 'Ecclesiam exaltare' versum est ibi in ecclesias spoliare." Whoever looks into the *Annals of the Four Masters*, under the years thus referred to, will find ample grounds for this remorse. Such sentences as, "Louth was laid waste by the Saxons," frequently meet the eye. Sword and flame were as unsparingly used on peasant, church, and homestead as in the days of the pagan Danes. Later, the sons or grandsons of those men found themselves treated as mere Irish by newer comers, who came preaching order but producing chaos. And of the many Englishmen who have so blundered in Ireland since then, how few have had the honesty of Giraldus to admit at the end that, in consequence of their meddling, the evil plight of everything had become worse.

About the same time, and alike in obedience to conscience, Giraldus wrote what he called his "Retractationes." But this tractate has little reference to Ireland, its chief object being to set himself right in the matter of certain libels which he had written against Hubert, Archbishop of Canterbury. He begins it with the appropriate old saying that "not to sin in anything is divine rather than human." He then proceeds to say: "I propose to set out here those things which are in my little works and which ought to be withdrawn, in order that the reader may beware and not take for certain things that are uncertain." On the part of a man who had made himself responsible for so many strange assertions, this mild opening, without self-accusation or regret, does not promise a rigorous or full examination of conscience. Scanty as the promise is, the performance is scantier still. The whole tractate extends to only a few pages, and more than half of it is occupied tendering to Hubert the most left-handed apology ever written. The editors remark that he might have made his retractation longer. Obviously—if he intended it to be complete. But if all he should have retracted, or should never have written, were withdrawn, the remnant of his works would be insignificant and worthless. Of this tractate of retractations so far as it relates to Ireland, Harris, the translator and editor of Ware's works, very justly says:—

"It is only a very slight apology for the many base scandals and invectives he had heaped together concerning Ireland in his *Topography*, many of which he confesses he had picked up only from that Publick Lyer, Common Fame, and yet has not remorse enough to disown them, concluding only that he would not for the most part affirm them, nor would he altogether deny them. Many Irish writers have published antidotes to some of the peculiar poisons of Cambrensis, but John Lynch, in a book entitled *Cambrensis Eversus*, has to some purpose taken him to pieces, and with a sharp and judicious pen exposed the numberless mistakes, falsehoods, and calumnies of that malicious writer."

Though no recantation can ever be fully effectual against falsehoods which have taken a place in literature, we Irish are as ready as other people to acknowledge that his recantation—tardy, reluctant, and inadequate as it is— redeems Giraldus's character somewhat. But there is no reason why we, alone of all mankind, should be blind to the collapse it constitutes. We can afford to say in our own humble fashion " May God forgive him his sins," but we are not obliged to go further and invest him with mitre and crozier in order to induce people to believe what he says of us. We are not obliged to give up Irish annalists who are generally as accurate as the sun for a stranger who is notoriously more changeable than the moon. The only special reason we have for treating him seriously is the fact that he was the first deliberate traducer of our people for the English market. As is his reputation for veracity, so are the Bulls. " I now dismiss thee, my Giraldus, who hast made for thyself a name big and bloated but not good."—White's *Apologia*, p. 18.

CHAPTER V.

Further Discussion of the Principal Instrument.

THE argument which gives most colour of probability to the *Laudabiliter*, which comes home most forcibly to everybody, and which has contributed more than anything else to convince people, is that arising from Adrian's nationality. It is most natural to suppose, and therefore people do suppose, that he was willing to strain a point in favour of the king of his native land, who, by a rare chance, had become King almost on the same day that he had become Pope. This contention is so extremely plausible that for many it constitutes in itself the very vitality of the *Laudabiliter*, and renders further inquiry unnecessary. It is dwelt upon in documents from which I have quoted, and in many which I have not mentioned; and, appealing as it does to the heart as well as to the reason, its enormous force cannot be denied. It is sustained by the fact that Henry, being then only twenty-three years of age, may be taken to have been still a comparatively pure youth, unstained by the crimes and vices of subsequent years, and might, conceivably, be deemed a suitable person to entrust with the performance of a good work. Plausible and forceful as the contention is, no sooner do we study it closely, even in admiration, than it becomes unsatisfactory. For, while admiring the supposed pure youth of twenty-three, we cannot keep out of our minds the question : Is the being a young layman of twenty-three a special qualification for the conversion of a people sunk in disgusting moral enormities? Would such an appointment, as one of the first acts of a new Pope, prove his sanity or insanity, which?

The assumption that Adrian wrote this or any other sweet letter to Henry is based upon an entire misconception of Adrian's character, knowledge, and experience. His life furnishes no reason in the world for thinking that he was a man subject to illusions or girlish emotions. If he had had them naturally, there is no reason, outside this document, to show that he carried them into the Chair of Peter. But outside this document there is no reason to think that he had them naturally in ruling force. Men who rise, as he did, from the lowest rank without extraneous aid, but by personal merit and force of character, must have, at starting, a fund of good sense, not of illusions. In their progress they acquire a great knowledge of human nature, and are generally able to judge the character of others and to control their feelings. This was Adrian's case, and he soon gave to the world a signal proof of his real character. The German Emperor, Frederick Barbarossa, at the head of a great army, was marching upon Rome with dubious intent. Adrian went with some attendants to meet him. The Emperor refused to give the usual salutation. Thereupon Adrian, the humblest of men, refused to give the kiss of peace. The Pope's attendants fled from the frowning faces of Frederick and his soldiers. Adrian remained alone but fearless. Alone he forced that stubborn Emperor to descend in presence of his proud soldiers and hold the stirrup for the Vicar of Christ. No matter what view anyone may take of the propriety of that transaction, the extraordinary courage, independence, and self-possession displayed by Adrian were such as would be extremely difficult to match in history. Yet these are the very qualities which the writing of the *Laudabiliter* would prove that he wholly lacked. One of the results of Adrian's having been born in Henry's dominions was that he had a better knowledge of Henry, and of the Plantagenet family generally, than if he had been born elsewhere. One of the consequences of this special knowledge was that he distrusted Henry, and *never wrote to him at all.* That is the conclusion to which my researches have led me. During his comparatively short pontificate Adrian issued as many Bulls and letters as any other Pope in a like time, most of them addressed to ecclesiastics, but some to the rulers of nearly every country in Europe. Migne's collection contains 258 of them, all characterised by good sense and piety, except the *Laudabiliter*, and that is the only one addressed to Henry, if it is addressed to him.

Nor is there any better foundation for the assumption, essential to belief in the *Laudabiliter*, that Adrian thought Ireland was a land of savages. He, in common with all educated men, knew that Ireland had sent to the Continent from the sixth century down to his own time a stream of missionaries eminent for learning, sanctity, and religious zeal, at times pouring them over Europe, as St. Bernard says, "like an inundation," and had thereby acquired the name of *Insula Sanctorum.* He himself had actually studied at Paris under an Irishman of that class, Mael-Muire, called on the Continent Marianus, a man whom he revered during his life. He knew in common with all men of sense that all the Marianuses had not gone out of Ireland, that many as able and as virtuous had remained at home devoting themselves to the service of God and of their own people, and that all had been educated in Ireland. Of some of these who had never left Ireland, and lived in his own time, the fame for sanctity was widespread and cannot have escaped his ears. Three Irishmen who lived in his own time are enrolled among the canonized Saints of the Catholic Church. He knew that the Irish had a regularly constituted hierarchy and body of clergy, that one of the Irish Bishops was a resident Legate of the Holy See, and that in 1152, only two years before his own accession, Cardinal Paparo had been in Ireland, had conferred pallia on the four Archbishops, and had presided over the Synod of Kells at which certain reforms were decided upon under his guidance. All this knowledge is utterly inconsistent with the assumption in the *Laudabiliter* that the Irish were savages outside the pale of Christianity and had forfeited the rights of freemen. Nor could indefinite and spasmodic accusations like those of Giraldus convince any sensible man that such was the case. If by any process he had been so convinced, he would have resorted to the methods of Popes before and since, consulted the Legate and the Irish Bishops, devised a rational remedy, and subsequently manifested an interest in its progress. He did not one of these things. If we are to believe the *Laudabiliter*, he discovered that the Irish had suddenly become savages, but fortunately he discovered at the same time an entirely new mode of reconverting them. Ecclesiastics were to be discarded and kept in the dark. The Irish were to be reconverted without knowing it; and that, too, by Henry Plantagenet, aged twenty-three. And the alleged author of this new plan, subsequently communicating with the Irish, not through Henry, but through the old channels, never inquired how the new plan was working. All this is so bad as to be simply untenable. But the writing of the *Laudabiliter* by Adrian would mean even worse than this. As read by its supporters, it would mean that he sold the liberties of the Irish people to Henry for as many *denarii* as there were houses in Ireland; and that the Irish people were, without accusation or trial, without excommunication, censure, or any of the ordinary preliminary steps, to be deprived by him of their liberties and made pay the price as well. This is just what Castlereagh did later, and we have no doubt what to think of him for it. There was not much resemblance between him and Pope Adrian.

No embassy, solemn or other, was sent by Henry to Rome to solicit from Pope Adrian a Bull relating to

Ireland. An embassy or mission consisting of Rotrodus, Bishop of Evreux, the Bishops of Lisieus and Le Mans, and the Abbot of St. Albans, was sent by Henry immediately after his accession, and its purposes are well known and perfectly intelligible. They were—(1) to pay the usual courtesy of congratulating a new Pope on his accession, a courtesy specially incumbent on Henry in this case, owing to the unprecedented circumstances that Adrian was the first Englishman who had become Pope, and that he had become Pope in the same year and in the same month in which Henry had become King; (2) to ask the Pope to release Henry from the obligation of a rash oath which he had made to his father; (3) to solicit the Pope's sanction for subjecting the Church in Scotland, and ultimately in the whole of the British Islands, to the jurisdiction of the English Archbishops. These objects are not specified in Henry's congratulatory letter which this embassy bore. They are gathered from other evidence no less cogent, and are not disputed. They were ample for the embassy, and in no place is there a word to suggest that there was any other object. John of Salisbury did not accompany this or any other embassy in any capacity, did not visit Pope Adrian until nineteen months after the date of this embassy, and therefore could have no ground for claiming as his own the work of the embassy. This is the embassy that is credited with having obtained the *Laudabiliter*. If John of Salisbury had accompanied it in an inferior position, as has been suggested, and if the embassy had obtained the *Laudabiliter*, his inferior position would not entitle him to say that he had obtained it by his own prayers. The request would have been that of the King, and even the Bishops and Abbot would hardly have arrogated it to themselves, much less he.

(1.) Henry's letter of congratulation,' to which the *Laudabiliter* is said to be the reply, occupies its proper place in the *Annales* of Baronius at the close of the year

1154. It eloquently expresses great joy, admiration, filial affection, and obedience; but it contains no petition, not a word about Ireland, and no acknowledgment of the Pope's sovereignty over islands; nor is there any other letter from Henry in which those subjects are mentioned. How the *Laudabiliter*, which is expressly concerned with those subjects, and *at the King's request*, can be an answer to this letter, which neither requests anything nor mentions them, is more than anyone not Bull-smitten can understand. Baronius does not insert the *Laudabiliter* after Henry's letter, where it should come if it were the answer and free from suspicion. Nor does he insert it in his regular narrative at all. But, after recording Adrian's death in 1159, he groups the *Laudabiliter* in an appendix of doubtful documents, some of which he expressly describes as fables, and for none of which he accepts any responsibility. He states that he derives it from the *Codex Vaticanus*, and that its condition is such that he cannot determine its correct date. Cardinal Moran, when residing at Rome, ascertained that the codex called by this name is a manuscript copy of the history of Matthew Paris, and that there is no Vatican copy, properly so called, of the *Laudabiliter* or of any of the Bulls we are considering, nor is there any original trace of one of them to be found at the Vatican. There is none but English authority for any of them. Matthew Paris was a monk of the thirteenth century, who copied and extended the *Chronica* of Roger de Wendover, a monk of St. Albans. The *Chronica* includes the Bull copied from Giraldus, who is, therefore, Baronius's ultimate authority.

(2.) We are not called upon to discuss the second purpose of the embassy.

(3.) Efforts, open and secret, were persistently made in the twelfth century by the English Archbishops to extend their jurisdiction over Scotland and the Isles; and their desire to include Ireland was no less real, though less openly avowed. For a long time it had been a traditional ambition of the See of Canterbury to extend its primatial jurisdiction over the whole of the British Islands, and thus form for itself a new patriarchate. Everything that favoured that project was welcome at Canterbury. The Danes or Ostmen of Dublin, Waterford, and Limerick, were slow in becoming Christians, and their paganism helped to delay their amalgamation with the Christian Irish. When, at length, they became Christians, that amalgamation was not complete. They regarded themselves as colonists in Ireland, and wished to have bishops of their own distinct from the Irish Bishops of the respective districts. Looking back now, we can easily see that theirs was a mistaken view, and that if Ireland was not their country they had no country. But they formed important and wealthy communities, and their desire was acceded to. In the case of each of those three cities they chose for their first bishop an Irishman; but they sent him to Canterbury to be consecrated. On subsequent occasions they selected an Irishman or one of their own race indifferently; but continued to have their bishops consecrated, and their priests ordained, at Canterbury. This entailed a duty of canonical obedience to Canterbury —exactly what Canterbury wanted. In this way, consciously or not, they were the first Unionists; from the Irish standpoint the first disruptionists. Their action was the first insidious element of disintegration introduced into the Irish nation, of which they had really become a part. When Henry II. came, his conquest, so far as it extended, gave him, according to the practice of the time, the right of nominating bishops to Sees; but the right acquired by conquest derived additional and irresistible force from the previous custom of the Danes. When, in subsequent years, this two-fold right had been confirmed by time, and by the unwavering loyalty of Dublin and Waterford to him, Henry had as full a power of nominating bishops for those cities, as for any other city in his dominions. Their sovereign beyond question, he needed no Papal or other enabling authority and had none. So long as he presented suitable men, his subject, the Archbishop of Canterbury, was bound to consecrate them, and was only too glad to do so. That this was the basis, the ample basis, of Henry's assumption of that power in Ireland, is clearly shown by what followed in his own and succeeding reigns. Had what is called a Bull been genuine, it would have been Henry's duty, and obviously his interest, to nominate a successor when the Primatial See of Armagh became vacant. It became vacant, and neither he nor anyone on his behalf attempted to interfere. Why? Because the power of his sword did not extend so far and he had no other power and did not claim to have any. On the very first vacancy of the See of Dublin he sent an Englishman to occupy that See, and that See continued to be occupied by Englishmen down to the time of the Reformation, I believe without a break. The same rule was long adhered to in Ferns and in Waterford. On the other hand, the seven successors of Gelasius in the See of Armagh were Irishmen, and the See of Cashel continued to be filled by Irishmen down to the time of the Reformation without a break. If the *Laudabiliter* had been genuine, and Henry's authority, he could have made no such distinction, because it makes none. It does not say that Armagh and Cashel were all right, and that it was only in Dublin and Waterford the rascals were. The moral is—no Bulls and no authority in Canterbury; and this is just the attitude the Irish Church has always maintained. Furthermore, had the *Laudabiliter* been genuine, its effect would have been to arm with the powers desired for the proposed patriarchate, not the Archbishop of Canterbury, but King Henry II.

The next argument, also, with which we have to deal is one of strong probability. It is the striking resemblance between the *Laudabiliter* and a Bull of Adrian's which is unquestionably genuine; proving, we are told, that both were written by Adrian. So far from denying this resemblance, I insist upon it, and invite the reader to judge whether it is not too close, and whether its effect is not to discredit instead of proving the *Laudabiliter*. The resemblance is so close and remarkable that it catches the eye on the most cursory glance through Adrian's letters. First of all, a resemblance could not in any case prove the *Laudabiliter*, and admirers of the Bulls are not wise in pressing it with that object; because, as already pointed out, a forged document always is made as like a genuine one as the forger can make it. To simulate the real and fortify itself with every element and circumstance of probability is of the very essence of forgery and almost a definition of that crime. Notwithstanding this, forgers failing to rid themselves completely of human frailty, their work is sometimes detected. It may even happen that excessive closeness to a model will betray them. Please pay special attention to a case in point and to another embassy or mission. This mission was sent to Adrian in 1158 by King Henry of England and King Louis of France jointly. While the letter or petition which it bore seems to have been signed by Louis only, Henry took the greater interest in the business, and the conduct of it was entrusted to a subject and great friend of his, the same Rotrodus, Bishop of Evreux, who had assisted at Henry's coronation, who had taken part in the mission of 1155, and who had made himself on various occasions useful to Henry. In short, the business was Henry's, but he, having no hope of obtaining at his own request the thing desired, induced Louis to lend his name. Pope Adrian was requested to issue a Bull sanctioning the proposed invasion of a country the initial letter alone of which is given in the Pope's reply. In this reticence the reply probably follows the petition, Rotrodus being present to explain what country *H.* signified. Collectors generally understand this *H.* to stand for *Hispania*, and they so expand it. Lately, however, it has been urged with much force that *Hibernia* was the country the invasion of which Adrian was asked to sanction. If that were so, it would of itself be conclusive proof that the *Laudabiliter* had not been obtained. As the discussion of that question would lead too far, I leave it open for a possible future occasion and proceed at a more modest level. Had Adrian been a man willing to sanction a proposed invasion at Henry's request—as the *Laudabiliter* implies—Henry would have no need of Louis's signature. Had Adrian been a man willing to grant such a Bull at the request of one king, he would more readily grant it at the request of two. Hence, while if the country to be invaded was Ireland this request itself would conclusively prove that the *Laudabiliter* had not been obtained, whatever may have been the country, the Pope's answer is of the highest interest to us. It is of two-fold interest: first, because it is an emphatic refusal; secondly, because the letter of refusal begins almost like the *Laudabiliter*, and is the same as the *Laudabiliter*, word for word, to the extent of several sentences, with the small but important difference that while the *Laudabiliter* is affirmative, the genuine letter is negative; while the *Laudabiliter* amounts to a cordial Yes, the genuine letter amounts to an emphatic No. There is even a resemblance in the reiteration of motives. That one was modelled on the other there is no room for doubting; the only question being whether this was done legitimately by an official scribe or illegitimately by a forger. The genuine refusal begins:—

  Satis Laudabiliter et fructuose de.

Our Bull begins:—

  Laudabiliter satis et fructuose de.

A few long sentences in the body of the letters are the
same, without even so much difference as is here notice-
able. This is obviously no case of a scribe's mechanical
adherence to a common form. No common form can ever
descend into the body and substance of an important and
independent document. To remove every possible pretence
of such a thing, there is not one other letter of Adrian's,
nor of any Pope's, so far as I have seen, beginning with
any of these words. One was modelled on the other. This
position is absolutely unassailable. Whoever has eyes
can see, whoever has ears can hear, that the genuine and
the false document are not merely alike, but to a large
extent identical, that there is no other Bull like them,
and that the substantial difference between them is that
one refuses what the other concedes. As this gives special
importance to the fact that the genuine letter is a refusal,
I quote so much from it as proves that fact and defines
the Pope's position. After urging some religious considerations, Pope Adrian says to Louis:—

"In addition to this, it seems to be neither prudent
nor safe to enter another country, unless the consent of
the princes and people of that country be first sought.
But you, as I understand, without having consulted the
clergy or princes of that country, propose to hasten
and to enter there. *This you should on no account attempt,*
unless you are first invited from thence on necessity
recognised by the princes of that country."

The genuine letter is, in its justness and firmness, exactly
what Adrian's other letters and his proved character would
lead us to expect from him. And what a different idea it
gives of him from that conveyed by the girlish conduct
of writing the *Laudabiliter* at the request of one of those
kings, or at the request of a private person. The resemblance in language is so close, the difference in sentiment
so great, that, in my opinion, the *Laudabiliter* instead of
being proved is utterly demolished. I have used many

arguments to the same effect, but whoever reads the *Satis Laudabiliter* will need no other argument, but will be convinced—(1) that the author of it was incapable of writing the *Laudabiliter*, and (2) that the *Laudabiliter*, by whomsoever written, was modelled on the *Satis Laudabiliter*. The forger had to omit Louis's name and forgot to insert Henry's. He had to omit the date, which did not suit him, and was unable to make up his mind about another date. And thus the *Laudabiliter* comes to us without name or date.

It has been asked with implied incredulity: "Are we to send to France for a model of forgery?" Even that might be thought worth doing. It is less than ten years since the manager of the *Times* newspaper confessed on oath, in a public court, that he had sent to France for forgeries and paid £2,500 for them. Henry had a far stronger interest, and had no need of such effort or expense. There was in his case no difficulty of any kind. He was himself ruler of, and spent most of his time in, part of the country now called France. The model Bull had been obtained by his friend, Bishop Rotrodus. Obtained mainly, if not solely, for Henry, he was of course familiar with its contents and phraseology, as were also his ministers. Where now is the suggested difficulty? Vanished.

Henry, doubting the loyalty of the first irregular invaders, came to Ireland at the head of a force capable of crushing both them and the Irish in the event of their combining against him. The effect was to strike them all with terror, and make them so civil that, to the extent to which he penetrated into the country, he achieved his purpose almost without striking a blow. While he stayed in the country Roderick O'Connor, devoid of courage and unsupported, kept out of range. So far as Henry was personally concerned, he effected his conquest by the sword, indeed, but by its flash and without bloodshed. So long as he remained in the country his absolute sovereignty could not be disputed except by the sword's edge, and this was not attempted. Knowing that he could not stay long in the country, he made the strongest bid in his power for the support of the clergy by causing, with the assistance of the Legate, a council of bishops and clergy to assemble at Cashel, and sending his trustiest clerical friends there to promise, on his behalf, the most liberal treatment for the Church, in fact the very rights and privileges which he had spent all his previous years in withholding from the Church wherever his power was strong enough. Proceeding by way of courteous invitation and entreaty, and not by imperative command, he succeeded in inducing many bishops to attend even from districts to which his army had not penetrated; and having got them together, the terms he offered, amounting to a millenium, were intended and calculated to make powerful friends for him. As soon as he and his military force had left the country, disorder broke out afresh on both sides. The invaders renewed their raids, and were, of course, resisted; and the conquest of Ireland, which had seemed almost complete in Henry's presence, dwindled down to the sea-port towns, with the adjacent districts and a few colonies, which had to pay tribute to the Irish for being allowed to remain in the country. This change produced a necessity for extraneous aid, Henry being unable to come again. Necessity being the mother of invention, brought forth on this occasion the *Laudabiliter*. The temptation to father it upon Adrian was irresistible. By a lucky chance he was an Englishman, and this, though weakening the moral force, would give a priceless air of probability —the first requisite for a forgery. Adrian being at the time long dead, if the *Laudabiliter* were mooted quietly without official proclamation, Adrian's successor might not hear of it, or hearing, might not feel called upon to repudiate a thing so informal. The sword of conquest having become weak, an inexpensive scheme, which promised to strengthen the hands that held it by combining the influence of a dead Pope with the divisions of the Irish, was in every way an admirable scheme. The *Laudabiliter* once launched in any way, it was impossible to recede without grave risk. True or false, it should then be stoutly upheld by every friend of the English in Ireland. To doubt it or allow it to be doubted might, at critical times, have imperilled the existence of English power in Ireland. To maintain it, whether true or false, was, therefore, a patriotic duty. So it would be regarded in the nineteenth century, as well as in the twelfth or thirteenth. Confirmatory Bulls soon seemed necessary, but such a fountain, once tapped, was not likely to run dry.

The ablest upholder of the disputed letters writes:—

"Donogh, son of Brian Boru, on being deposed by the Irish princes had gone to Rome in the previous century, carrying with him, it is said, the insignia of royalty and power, and transferred, before his death there, the sovereignty of Ireland to the Roman See."

What an extraordinary story! Another wooden leg for the Bull. One would suppose there were already too many. First it was Constantine the Great who gave the power. The document in that case was forged, and Constantine had no power over Ireland. Now it is Donogh O'Brien; and admire the present he gives to the Pope—the sovereignty of Ireland, of which the Irish have stripped him. This was more than regal liberality. Under Irish, as, indeed, under any law, a reigning king had no power to transfer his kingdom to a foreigner. Here we have a deposed king doing it. Of course, the story deserves no consideration except for fun. I will content myself with one quotation on the subject from Dr. Lanigan's *Ecclesiastical History*, Vol. IV., page 146:—

"Neither in any of the Irish annals nor in the

ecclesiastical documents of those times, whether Roman or Irish, is there a trace to be found of the transfer of Ireland to Urban II. or to any Pope of that or a preceding period by either Irish kings or Irish nobility."

Another witness invoked to support the Bulls is Peter of Blois; but he makes no response to the call. Like Robert de Monte, he stands mute. He lived and wrote later than Giraldus, spent part of his youth in the regular employment of Henry II., and afterwards willingly rendered occasional services to that king. A copy of the *Laudabiliter* is found among his manuscripts, as are also copies of letters from the Emperor Frederick and other persons with whom Peter had no connection. When or by whom they were placed there, and whether Peter ever saw them, no one knows. Then he gives no support to the *Laudabiliter?* None whatever. Such evidence as his writings afford tends exactly the other way. If the *Laudabiliter* were, as is alleged, known by him to be genuine, he was just the man who would not fail to include among Henry's titles one derived from Ireland. In his letters written in 1177, 1182, and later, and in his dedication of a "*Compendium in Job*," he addresses Henry elaborately as "Most Illustrous King of England, Duke of Normandy and Aquitaine, Count of Anjou," but gives no title arising from Ireland.

In 1317 Pope John XXII. addressed a letter to King Edward II. of England, remonstrating strongly with him on certain intolerable wrongs, of which, he said, the Irish had complained to him, John, and appending a copy of the *Laudabiliter* made from the history of Matthew Paris. He did this in consequence of what is called an Irish Remonstrance addressed to him in 1315, in which the *Laudabiliter* is expressly admitted. On one side, this admission is held to be conclusive of its authenticity, while on the other an attempt has been made to explain it away as having been made merely for the sake of argument, and by way of striking the English with their own weapon. If it were an admission conceded for that purpose, no question of its correctness could affect its force. The admission may have been so intended, for the Remonstrance is strongly argumentative. But, as it stands, the admission seems to be absolute. Disregarding the assertions on both sides, I will place the reader in a position to judge.

The Remonstrance is addressed in this manner:—

"To the Most Holy Father in Christ the Lord, John, by the grace of God, Supreme Pontiff, from his devoted children Donald Oneyle, King of Ulster, and by hereditary right, true heir of the whole of Hibernia, also the petty kings and magnates of the same country, and the Hibernian people."

The Remonstrators say that as the Pope hears from the English much that is false and viperous, and very little that is true about the Irish people, they desire to correct the balance in that respect. In manly and indeed somewhat excessively forcible language, they direct the Pope's attention to the long and glorious history of Ireland before the time of King Leoghaire, in whose reign Pope Celestine sent St. Patrick to Ireland, and from whom Donald is descended in direct line; they point out how devoted to the religion of Christ Ireland afterwards became; and so they proceed to the passage in which we are concerned, and of which the following is a translation:

"At length Pope Adrian, your predecessor, an Englishman more even by affection and choice than by origin, in the year of our Lord, 1172, on a suggestion of iniquity, false and foul, made by Henry, King of England, under whom, and perhaps by whom, in the same year, as you know, St. Thomas of Canterbury suffered death for the sake of justice, and the defence of the Church, moved by English predilection, and wholly omitting all order and law, in fact improperly conferred the dominion of our country upon him whom for the aforesaid crime he ought rather to have deprived of his own kingdom. Alas! he relaxed his pastoral watchfulness, and thus, depriving us of our rightful country, without any fault of ours, and without cause, delivered us to be torn by the cruel teeth of all beasts."

The Remonstrance then describes at great length what the conduct of the English in Ireland had been, and contrasts it with the professions by which it was supposed the Bull had been obtained, thus showing how grossly they had abused the trust reposed in them by Pope Adrian, and *how just and agreeable to Adrian's precedent it would be to issue a fresh Bull conferring the sovereignty of Ireland upon Edward Bruce as the Irish then desired.*

This last clause gives the explanation of the whole Remonstrance, and renders it quite immaterial whether the admission in it was made positively or only arguendo. The document is substantially the work of Scotch adherents of Bruce, desirous of obtaining Ireland for their master and themselves, and willing to bring the English tradition into their service. Bruce approved of it, as he would have approved of anything that promised him assistance; and obviously it had greater force presented in the name of the Irish, whether with or without their consent, than if presented in Bruce's own name. Bruce could not have presented it in his own name with any hope of success; first, because he had no right in the matter; secondly, because Pope John did not like the Bruces, and distinctly says so. The document is clearly the work of Bruce's party, and further confirmation of this will be noticed in the incorrect spelling of proper names, in the numerous historical anachronisms of which no Irish scholar would have been guilty in relation to his own country, and in the admission of Adrian's Bull, which, as we shall presently see, the Irish at that time firmly denied. And if this Remonstrance had been the work of Irishmen, they would have preserved a copy of it with the other memorials of that time. The absence of copy or record of it by Irish writers shows that they had neither act nor part in it, and probably not even knowledge of it. To find it one has to search in the *Scotichronicon*, Fordun's Latin History of Scotland. It occurs in Thomas Hearne's edition of that work, Vol. III., beginning on page 908.

Having demolished what was described as Irish evidence for the Bulls, I cannot do better than produce evidence from the English settlers in Ireland against them. In the year 1325, that is, only ten years after the date of the Remonstrance, a letter was sent to the Pope, not by Scotchmen, nor yet by Irishmen, but by sworn friends of these so-called Bulls. It was sent under seal by the Lord Justiciary and the Royal Council of the English Pale in Ireland, and was presented to the Pope by William of Nottingham, canon and precentor of St. Patrick's Cathedral, Dublin. In this document some stale charges are repeated against the Irish, with this interesting addition, that they are described as—

"Asserentes etiam Dominum Regem Angliae ex falsa suggestione et ex falsis bullis terram Hiberniae in dominium impetrasse, ac communiter hoc tenentes: They also assert that our lord the King of England obtained dominion over the land of Ireland by a false suggestion and by false Bulls, and they commonly hold this opinion."

Against the admission made in the Remonstrance through the mouth of Scotchmen, we have here a positive statement made in the most solemn manner, under their own seal, by the English in Ireland, whose interest it was not to make this statement, that the Irish commonly held the Bulls to be false. This important document was discovered in the Barberini Archives in Rome, in the course of a search instituted by Cardinal Moran for authentic documents relating to Irish affairs in those centuries. An exhaustive search in those and other Papal archives, the contents of which have never been printed, would solve many an otherwise difficult problem, and correct many an erroneous opinion. Furthermore, it is manifest that if the English possessed real Bulls they would on such an occasion have produced them as the most thorough and conclusive mode of confounding the Irish and settling for ever the question of true or false. Instead of doing this, they sent a whine to Rome.

Gentlemen could easily prove the authenticity of these Bulls if allowed to argue illogically: to prove the antecedent by the subsequent and the subsequent by the antecedent, but not one of them independently. Anything, true or false, could be proved if that were proof. It is a method never resorted to in a good cause. The ablest supporter of these Bulls resorts to it, and without proving any one of the documents uses each in turn to prove the others. For instance, he says that Adrian's letter is proved by Alexander's confirmation, affects to think that settles the matter, and rides off with an air of satisfaction, leaving both unproved. He says that Adrian believed in Constantine's donation, and in proof thereof points to the *Laudabiliter*, a document as impossible to prove as the spurious donation itself and for the same reason. What this mode of arguing really does prove is, that there are no better arguments, and that if logic be insisted upon the Bulls must be abandoned. With this plan the same writer combines another for proving the Bulls, if you please, and in order to make it clear and at the same time to show that I do him no injustice, I must quote a whole paragraph from his essay:—

"We would further claim special attention for the following consistorial decree, made in June, 1558, at the time when Ireland was raised to the dignity of a kingdom. It was subsequently embodied in a Bull by Pope Paul IV.:—' Whereas ever since *the dominion of Ireland was obtained from the Apostolic See* by the Kings of England, they always had styled themselves only Lords of Ireland, till Henry VIII., breaking away from the unity of the Catholic Church and obedience to the Roman Pontiff, usurped the kingly title,' etc. This document alone is sufficient to prove the privilege of Adrian. What reply is made to it by the learned impugners of the privilege? Why this, that Pope Paul IV. wrote only what was suggested to him by Philip and Mary. Comment is unnecessary."

Quite so; comment is unnecessary. The reply of the impugners is the reply of reason. The fact that the Pope had not the *Laudabiliter* before him, but was prompted, is clear on the face of the writing just quoted. It attributes to the *Laudabiliter* a transference of dominion—a thing not in that document. That transference was an English tradition. Whence did the Pope derive it? Not from the *Laudabiliter*, for it is not there. Queen Mary's cousin, Cardinal Pole, an Englishman, was at the moment soliciting favours from the Pope for Philip and Mary. The information in question would have been the strongest reason he could urge upon the Pope for granting one of the favours he was asking. Cardinal Pole as an Englishman probably believed the information to be true. There was, therefore, absolutely, no reason for withholding it, and he had a strong actual reason for conveying it to the Pope. We are seriously asked to believe that he, without cause, omitted to convey the information, and that the Pope, instead of deriving the information from the living voice of Cardinal Pole present with him, searched back among the dusty papers of four hundred years until he found, in a document in which it *is not*, a reason which Pole had all the time on the tip of his tongue and would not express. This bare statement of the case renders comment quite unnecessary; a reader who could not do the rest ought to give up reading.

Assuming that the information was given by Pole in

good faith, it was none the less in the interest of Philip and Mary. That the Catholic King of Spain and the Catholic Queen of England combined, and represented by Cardinal Pole, would have been powerful prompters needs no demonstration from me; it is self-evident.

Passing over the suggested race between the Pope and Henry VIII. to confer upon Ireland in the sixteenth century a dignity—if it be such—which it had enjoyed at least a thousand years before, the paragraph just quoted, like much that is written in support of these Bulls, in addition to expressly claiming and assuming much that cannot be conceded, is calculated to effect still more than it openly expresses. Its ostensible purpose is to convey a sweeping denial that Philip and Mary had prompted the Pope. We now know what to think of that. Its real and greater effect is not this apparent one, but to capture the reader's conviction by assuming his assent to a proposition implied but not stated, which would silence all opposition for ever more, but which is so far from being sustainable that no one will venture openly to submit it to argument: the proposition, namely, that once a Pope has based a Bull on a preceding Bull that preceding Bull, even if forged, must then be regarded as genuine. The writer does not state this in so many words; no one will venture to do so; but turn back to the quoted paragraph and say is not that the idea it conveys. Yes, and that is the sense in which the writer himself towards the end of the same essay refers back to that paragraph. Now, why convey to the mind of the ordinary reader an idea so wrong that it will not bear to be stated in its nakedness? Why, but to gain some shade, however transient, for documents which are being shrivelled up by the sun of truth. Genuine documents never need such contrivances. Having first bid for the reader's confidence by expressly admitting that the question is purely historical, the writer casually raises across the inquirer's path a bar marked

"No thoroughfare." How is the historical inquirer to proceed if there is no thoroughfare? The claim that Pope Paul's Bull by itself is sufficient to prove the authenticity of a document written four hundred years before can mean no less than that all statements in Bulls are infallible, that even a spurious Bull can be rendered genuine at any subsequent date, and that this having been done it is irreligious to doubt the *Laudabiliter*. If that were so, it would be more irreligious to doubt Constantine's donation, which, though more frequently confirmed than the *Laudabiliter* has been, everyone knows to be false. An imposture in the beginning, it remained an imposture after all confirmations. Holy men did not think themselves debarred from doubting it, did not think the inquiry closed by all the confirmations, did not consider comment unnecessary, but on the contrary continued scraping it until they succeeded in revealing its falseness to all men, Popes included. This is just what Irishmen have been doing since they first heard of these Bulls, just what they are doing now; and we are similarly entitled to have this pseudo-religious bar removed from our path. To erect it is to confess fear of inquiry, and inability to support the *Laudabiliter* by fair means. There are other instances of the recognition of the *Laudabiliter* by the Pope, to which supporters of that document triumphantly point, but to which all the reasoning in this paragraph applies. In noticing them this reasoning will be understood, in addition to any that may be peculiar to them.

In 1570 the then Archbishop of Cashel was in Spain, seeking assistance for the Irish Catholics against the tyranny of Queen Elizabeth, and Cardinal Alciato, writing to him, remarks that—" It is well known that the kingdom of Ireland belongs by feudal right to the Church." This extraordinary statement is called a proof of the *Laudabiliter* by an Irishman who knows, as all know, that the claim it embodies never was well known, nor known at all, and is pure fiction. We are not in the least concerned with what the Cardinal was thinking of; it is sufficient that he wrote nonsense. If writings of that sort can be held to prove anything, or are worth pursuing, the greatest number of them will be found to have been issued in connection with the Confederation of Kilkenny, about the middle of the seventeenth century. This is an uncomfortably late date for people who attach any value to such confirmations; for although it is universally and always true that no power in Church or State can ever render genuine that which was originally false, the lapse of time makes this fact more obvious. If a forged document of the twelfth century could have been rendered genuine in the thirteenth or fourteenth, it could equally well be rendered genuine in the seventeenth. Yet, when a date so familiar is named, we ask why not in the nineteenth, and why need friends of these Bulls be uneasy if what they desire can be done even now? This is the logical result of their claiming that anything subsequent *could* render genuine a false Bull. References to subsequent events, ancient or modern, have no meaning unless they amount to that claim. On amounting to that claim they become simply ridiculous. If you cannot prove your Bull true on its birthday, you can never afterwards make it true. That which was originally spurious cannot by lapse of time become genuine. If there be any purpose for which it is useful, it can only be the detection of its author.

Innocent X., in his instructions to the Nuncio Rinuccini, says:—

"Ireland recognised no supreme prince save the Roman Pontiff; and Henry II., King of England, desiring to subjugate Ireland, had recourse to Adrian: from that Pontiff, who was an Englishman, he obtained with a liberal hand all that he asked. The zeal manifested by Henry in wishing to convert all Ireland to the Faith induced Adrian *to bestow on him the dominion of that land.*"

What all these unfounded sayings do prove beyond yea
or nay is, what we had known without them, that when
Cardinals, Popes, and even Saints write on secular subjects
of which they have no personal knowledge, they are as
liable as other men writing on hearsay to be misled, and
in the instances quoted were, in fact, flagrantly misled,
and induced to state what was and remains historically
untrue, and what the gentlemen who quote these passages
know to be untrue. The Irish never recognised the Pope as
temporal sovereign, and never were asked to do so. They
did not wait for Henry II. to convert them to the Faith,
as Innocent X. ought to have known. The Bull *Laudabiliter* does not confer dominion, as is evident to all who
read it, such as it is. The Pope's office is no sinecure. Few
public men have more calls upon their attention than the
occupant of that office. To concentrate his own mind
upon them all is an utter impossibility. No one will, with
a serious face, suggest that the Popes, on those occasions,
instituted a special inquiry, or any inquiry, into the
authenticity of the *Laudabiliter*. They had more sensible
and important work to do than would be such an
investigation without cause. And besides, the Pope is
not *ex-officio* an expert in history any more than he is
in astronomy. On many subjects, if he acts at all, he must
of necessity rely upon the statements of other persons who
profess to know, as in sickness he relies upon the opinion
of his doctor. Those other persons may err in malice or
in good faith. The difference is immaterial to my argument. Popes have accepted and embodied in public
documents certain statements about Ireland which are
untrue. Does that make them true? Is not its effect
exactly the opposite? Does it not prove to demonstration
that those Popes relied upon hearsay and were deceived?
How can that fact help the Bulls? Just suppose an
analogous case: Suppose it were conveyed to the Pope,
on the authority of an eminent statesman of the present

day, that the Irish were Hottentots, and the Pope, accepting the assurance in simple faith, on what ought to be reliable authority, issued a Bull stating, as a well known fact, that our skins were as black as the raven's wing. According to the principle of those who hold that such a "confirmation" alters the laws of nature, we should immediately and thenceforward be all black, though our colour underwent no change whatever. That is the method of historical investigation essential to the alleged Bulls.

Some other persons besides those dealt with have been from time to time *named* as giving support to the *Laudabiliter*, but no words of theirs to that effect have been cited. Why? Because there are none to cite. Having myself taken the trouble to examine them all and found that they give no support to the instrument, I dismiss them as so many unwilling witnesses called in vain to make an array of empty names for people who lack arguments. The impartial reader must long ago have become conscious of the fatal mistake friends of the *Laudabiliter* have made in providing it with so many props. It is hard to know what else to do but prop a thing that totters. Yet I feel certain that their success would have been greater and more lasting if they had been content with arguments fewer in number, but better chosen and consistent with each other. Having no leg of its own to stand upon in the shape of an authentic original, confirmatory Bulls became necessary, and with lapse of time other supports, until it came to pass that the unfortunate *Laudabiliter* has had at different times probably a hundred wooden legs applied to it, most of them left ones. The simplest of us can see that legs for which nature is responsible, are usually made in pairs of left and right, to work in such a manner as not to jostle still less to destroy each other; and we can have no doubt that the advocates of this centipede Bull would be very glad and relieved from much of their perplexity if they could procure two legs for it, or even one, of the right sort. We have examined, and I think smashed, all the legs of any substance. Dr. Zinkeisen, with full knowledge of them all, says in the *English Historical Review* for October, 1894: "The Bull *Laudabiliter*, which has long been considered by many a genuine Bull of Adrian IV., must now, I think, be considered an innocent forgery, a mediaeval scholastic exercise." The innocence or guilt of this particular forgery, as of all others, must depend upon whether it was intended to have any operation, and whether the work containing it was intended to be regarded as history or as fiction.

Had the Bull been genuine it would have been known in 1167 to the learned Bishop of St. David's, and he would have prompted Dermot Mac Murrough to urge it upon Henry as the most powerful inducement for the purpose they had in view. It would have been known in 1170 to Strongbow, when he found it necessary to go to the Continent to induce Henry to allow the Irish campaign to proceed. On neither of these occasions was it used or mentioned. It would have been known to St. Laurence O'Toole in 1171, when his efforts to unite the Irish for the expulsion of the invaders proved that he was unaware of its existence. Those efforts gained for him Henry's enmity. They would have gained for him a censure from the Pope if the *Laudabiliter* had been genuine. Instead of censure, the Pope conferred on him every mark of confidence and favour. In 1178, as Laurence and five other Irish Bishops were passing through England on their way to Rome to attend the Council of Lateran, Henry was so suspicious and felt his cause to be so unsound that he had them all arrested and detained until, as Ussher says, "they were all, in order to obtain permission to proceed, forced to swear that they would do nothing at Rome to the detriment of the King or of his kingdom." Although an oath obtained under durance could have imposed little obligation, they probably kept it, which is more than Henry would have done. Henry, whom no oath could bind, unable to believe that they had kept theirs, stopped Laurence on the return journey, and according to Giraldus, had him detained in Normandy until he died there; and this although Laurence had with him on that occasion a genuine Bull from the Pope of a very different character from the Bulls we are discussing, and had been appointed the Pope's Legate for the whole of Ireland. This contrast between the treatment accorded to Laurence by the Pope and by Henry must be taken to be the practical expression of their respective opinions of Laurence. If that be so, the Pope had confidence in Laurence, and none in Henry; and Laurence having no knowledge of the *Laudabiliter*, it follows that the Pope had none. And this is confirmed by the genuine Bull then given to Laurence, which contains nothing about the *Laudabiliter*, nor about any power conferred upon Henry, nor about Irish vices. Every fact tends irresistibly to show that no one except Government agents had any knowledge of the *Laudabiliter* until it appeared in Giraldus's works about 1189--that is, thirty-four years after its supposed date. Adrian, Alexander, John of Salisbury, and King Louis were then dead, and all danger of repudiation was over.

The wilful exposure of a curious phenomenon is generally understood to be an invitation to the public to observe it. It is a curious phenomenon that from the first day to the last everyone who has attempted to give credit to the *Laudabiliter* has, at the same time, attempted to enlarge its scope. Not one of its supporters, ancient or modern, has been content with its text, as given by Giraldus. Every man, without exception, who has so far undertaken to maintain the *Laudabiliter* has either altered its text or represented it as containing what it does not contain. The earliest instance is the passage in the

Metalogicus. Next comes the first of those letters attributed to Alexander. Right away down the whole course of its history since then the writings and the traditions intended to sustain the *Laudabiliter* have magnified and exaggerated that instrument, spurious as it is. This is more than a curious phenomenon. It is a grave offence. It would be so regarded in business. It would be a grave offence even if the instrument were genuine. Is the offence of amending a forgery less grave? If anyone who rejects the letter were to commit a like offence, not alone would he be promptly and severely condemned, but his attempt would be set up as a new proof of the *Laudabiliter.* Is tampering with it in the opposite sense less a proof of its falsity?

Mr. Richey, in his lectures delivered in Trinity College, Dublin, inserts in the *Laudabiliter* these imperious words: "That you do enter and take possession of that land." These are not in it as given by any author but himself. Where did he get them? With what object does he interpolate them? He interpolates them with the same old object for which the *Laudabiliter* was first written—to unite the Pope's name with England's sordid political purpose. Whoever supports the *Laudabiliter* promotes that object, whether consciously or unconsciously. So others also insert words not in the *Laudabiliter* as given by Giraldus, and speak of that document as "Pope Adrian's letter of grant." One who takes liberties with the text can make it a letter of grant or a letter of anything else he likes. But there are people who think that such treatment invalidates a document and discredits the holder. Some writers who give the text correctly furnish it with a descriptive heading, the description being false by excess. These arts of twisting, straining, and altering are not edifying, and do not impart strength. At the very least, they betray a consciousness that the document is defective as it stands. People who say that a document is authentic should first agree among themselves as to what the document is, and in what form it can be shown to be authentic. Giraldus is their highest authority for the text of this document; yet they are not satisfied with the text he has given them, but alter it as danger threatens.

We have now completed our study of his text, and of all the arguments worth noticing that ever have been advanced in support of it. It is sufficiently obvious that the result is fatal, not to it alone, but to the letters bearing Alexander's name, which we have noticed incidentally. These we will next consider more directly, but briefly.

CHAPTER VI.

The other Instruments considered. All found to be spurious.

THE five Bulls or letters we are considering constitute a set with the common object of promoting the English interest in Ireland. That being so, any taint affecting one of them affects all. One being vitiated, all are vitiated. One being false, all are false. If the first is false, as I think we have found it to be, the discredit of the remainder is consequential. The second necessarily falls to the ground, even if written by Pope Alexander's own hand, since what it imports to confirm is itself false. Once a forgery always a forgery. Even if the Pope and the Irish were to unite in calling it genuine it would still remain spurious. This then is my first point with reference to the first of these letters ascribed to Alexander—even if rightly so ascribed it would be invalid. Popes have, as I have shown, acted upon a forged instrument; but they did not thereby make it valid. It remained false, and every act based upon it was to that extent invalid *ab initio.*

But Pope Alexander did not confirm the *Laudabiliter*, and did not write these letters nor any of them. The forged document which I have shown that Popes acted upon was a forged Imperial document purporting to belong to an age many hundreds of years gone by. It was not a Papal Bull, still less a Bull of the immediately preceding Pope, still less a Bull of yesterday. That was too near for deception, and too near for the success of the old spurious donation to form a precedent. It would be the business of the Pope and his officials to know Papal documents so recent. We have in this case the best possible guarantee that the business was discharged. The man whom we call Pope Alexander III. was, in 1155, as Cardinal Roland, Chancellor to Pope Adrian IV., and it is through his hands the *Laudabiliter* should have passed to be genuine. First, then, he had personal knowledge of the fact that Adrian had not issued the *Laudabiliter*, and therefore he did not write this first letter. Secondly, this first letter confirms a grant of the dominion of Ireland, a thing which the *Laudabiliter* does not contain, a thing which Alexander would have known from memory and from the document before him that it did not contain, and therefore he did not write this first letter. On this double ground this first letter is spurious.

The succession of Adrian's Chancellor to the Papacy made the floating of the *Laudabiliter* more difficult than it would otherwise have been, and perhaps explains why it was not proclaimed, and also why Henry was disposed to favour Alexander's rival the anti-Pope.

As in the case of Adrian, we must consider briefly Alexander's character and his knowledge of Henry. The English Catholic historian, Lingard, thought those Bulls were genuine, admitted that Alexander was quite aware of Henry's duplicity and notoriously immoral life, and expressed his opinion that Alexander must have smiled at the hypocrisy of such a character as Henry undertaking to evangelize Ireland. So much light has been thrown upon the whole subject since Dr. Lingard wrote that if he were living now he could no longer entertain that opinion. For my part I think it was strange and absolutely untenable when written; and it cannot be maintained for a moment now. Apart from these wretched letters, there is nothing in Alexander's whole life to justify such an opinion. To knowingly address a corrupt and unreliable man as one inspired by God for a holy purpose, to arm him with authority of unlimited range, and to smile at the whole as a good joke, would make the Pontiff guilty of far graver hypocrisy than Henry's, and would be a gross abuse of his office, such as there is no warrant whatever for allowing. I have had occasion already to indicate that Alexander was a very different man from what all this would imply. Before becoming Pope he had occupied a position which enabled him to study Henry closely in his relations with the Church. He was no less cognisant of those relations during Adrian's pontificate than during his own. Information given to Adrian was practically given to him. He came to his new office, not as a stranger, but in possession of the full heritage of knowledge. This knowledge was not calculated to inspire him with confidence in Henry. When the test came Henry favoured Alexander's rival so far as he thought his interests permitted him to do so. This was not calculated to increase Alexander's confidence in him. Alexander once established, Henry sent him congratulations and offerings in gold. The congratulations were accepted; the gold was declined. The reason is not stated, but it can hardly have been one flattering to Henry. After a few days the gold was offered again. It was then accepted, as though purified by the preceding rebuff. Thomas à Becket and John of Salisbury were subjects and capable students of Henry: and though courteous to him, they knew him too well to trust him. This can easily be gathered from their letters to Alexander. They complain of Henry's ambition to become absolute master of everything within his own dominions, and of his alternate resistance to, and evasion of, Papal interference; in short, of his disloyalty to the See of Rome. Knowing that he could not become absolute master of the Church in England so long as it continued to form part of a universal Church, Henry was quite willing to reduce it to national dimensions by severing the connection with Rome if he found a suitable season and a sufficient number of churchmen upon whom he could rely. Everyone knew this. In Protestant England it is made a merit of Henry's, and he is regarded as a "Reformer" born prematurely. All this concerned the Pope directly and intimately, and no man in Europe had a better knowledge of it than he. And apart from these questions which touched his own office, Alexander must have been at least as cognisant as other men of the reputation Henry had at this time established for himself as an adulterer, a breaker of his oath, a seller and delayer of justice, a hammer of the Church, a threatened schismatic, an incipient heretic, a contingent Mahommedan. If all the other evidence which I have urged and am about to urge were obliterated, I should still be unable in the presence of this single paragraph to believe that Alexander addressed this man as a devoted son of the Church inspired by God for the conversion of the Irish.

In 1170 King Henry II., desiring to partition his dominions amongst his sons, summoned a council of bishops and clergy in London, and intimated that he desired his son Henry to be annointed and crowned King of England. This crowning of an heir during his father's lifetime was a thing that had never been done in England before, and such ill success attended it that it has not been repeated. Thomas à Becket, Archbishop of Canterbury, being at the time in forced exile, the English bishops were under orders from him, and also from the Pope directly, to take no part in the proposed coronation, as it was a function specially attached to the See of Canterbury, and the performance of it by any other bishop in the existing circumstances would amount to taking the side of the King against Thomas. Notwithstanding this, "Roger, Archbishop of York, regardless of justice, throwing aside the fear of God, and contemning the prohibition of our lord the Pope," obeyed Henry and crowned the young King. Thereupon Pope Alexander suspended Roger, and also the Bishop of Dunelm, excommunicated the Bishops of London and Salisbury, and wrote strong letters to all of them complaining that "We are sometimes obliged to extend the rod of discipline against those whom we ought to have as helpers for the correction of others." These letters show the relations between the Church and Henry as anything but harmonious, and they show Alexander holding his own with courage and tenacity, and standing like a man by the exiled Thomas when the bishops, Thomas's own countrymen, had deserted him and given way to Henry.

There is a curious little plea, in itself not worth noticing, but as it is forced upon us as a proof of these letters we may as well look at it as one of the trifles that are turned to that use. Alexander addressed Henry as "Dearest Son in Christ;" therefore, we are told, he had a special affection for Henry. It is manifest that he addressed Henry and other Kings so because that was the form in which Popes had been accustomed to address Christian Kings, just as "Your Most Gracious Majesty" is the recognised form in which one ought to address Queen Victoria, whether she is gracious or not. Every age and rank has its own forms of courtesy, which must be adhered to so long as communication is maintained. This form of address had no more significance when applied to Henry than when applied to any other King, no more than "Your humble servant" at the end of our letters. In the letters of no Pope is this shown more clearly than in Alexander's, and in none of Alexander's is it shown more clearly than in those addressed to Henry. It begins letters containing the strongest censure as well as those containing none. It is the form of address used in some strong letters from which I have quoted, and in a further letter in which he says—"Your obduracy against justice, and against our desire for your welfare, we can endure no longer." In his letters to Becket also, though mentioning Henry in the same terms of formal endearment, he complains no less bitterly for that. In one of them he writes despairingly of the length of time he has waited in kindness and patience for the return of Henry to a sense of his duty, and how after smooth and sweet words he has had to resort to hard and rough words, and even to threats of extreme measures if their property and their freedom of action were not restored to the Church and its ministers. The " Dearest Son in Christ" is nothing more than a form of courtesy, and does not indicate either affection or weakness. Used in genuine letters, it could not be departed from in forged ones. Alexander's relations with Henry were one sustained manifestation of courage and independence. For thirteen years most of his letters to Henry are burdened with demands, complaints, threats. The struggle between Church and King culminated in the murder of the Archbishop of Canterbury at the altar. Thereupon, according to these Bulls, Alexander's heart softened; he poured out upon Henry a torrent of affection so long dammed up, yielded all he had spent so many years withholding, and then—mark—his heart is suddenly dried up again, so that after these letters relating to Ireland he never writes another friendly letter to Henry. To accept the Bulls one must believe all this.

It is, to be sure, pleaded that "his acquittal at Avranches in August, and his submission, reinstated him in Alexander's favour." If so, how is it that in all the years that followed Alexander never wrote to Henry in that sense, except in these wretched letters? I maintain that he never wrote to Henry at all after the murder of Becket. In Migne's collection Alexander's letters to Henry before the date of the murder are given in full, and their dates and substance leave no doubt as to the times at which they were written. After the date of the murder there are scattered through Migne's collection a few letters from Alexander to Henry, but incomplete, without date, and with the heading "Intra, 1159-1181." That is a period of over twenty years, at any point of which they may have been written, if genuine. The only letters from him to Henry that are given in full after the date of the murder are—these letters relating to Ireland and one other which Migne himself places under the heading SPURIA. Is it not a remarkable and unfortunate coincidence that it is to "Henry, King of the English," the letter is addressed, which Migne, with no interest to serve but that of truth, feels constrained to brand as spurious? Is it not a further remarkable and unfortunate coincidence that this spurious letter, like modern copies of the *Laudabiliter*, is dated at *Rome*, where the Pope was *not* at the time at which it purports to have been written? Here is the date in full: "Given at Rome, the eleventh day of the month of December, and first year of our pontificate:" that is, 11th December, 1159. This same volume of Migne contains a genuine letter written by Alexander on that very day at the place where he *did* reside! All this is so interesting to friends and foes of our precious Bulls that a reader of either class will like to know the purport of this spurious letter. It is as kind to Henry as he could desire, and represents the Pope as taking Henry's side strongly against "Thomas, Archbishop of Canterbury." Now, Thomas did not become Archbishop for three years after that date. This mistake of the forger led to the detection of the forgery, and greater care was taken in subsequent efforts of that kind. In this letter the Pope is made to say of Thomas:—"We degrade him from every ecclesiastical order and from the episcopate, and declare him an idiot; and we command you, under pain of major excommunication, to impose this condign punishment upon him—namely, to shut him up in the prison of a monastery, where he shall perform perpetual penance." This is the kind of Bull Henry's courtiers were ready to provide for his convenience. It would be impossible to conceive anything more directly opposed to Alexander's real attitude. The concoction of this Bull was a more audacious act than the concoction of those we are considering. But the motive was nearly the same. Were the gentlemen who did it too virtuous to write those we are considering?

Let us look for a moment at what is called an acquittal of Henry. It looks more like the Scotch verdict of Not Proven. On the Sunday before Lady Day in August, 1172, at Mass in the Cathedral of Avranches, before two Legates, an assembly of bishops and priests, and a large congregation of people, Henry swore on the Holy Gospels that he was innocent of the murder of Becket, deeply regretted that crime, and would, within certain specified dates, perform certain specified penances for having uttered the rash expression, in obedience to which the murder had been committed. One of these penances was that he should immediately restore, absolutely, and without diminution, its freedom and its property to the See of Canterbury, and to the Church generally. Another was that he should regard his kingdom as forfeited, and should, there and then, become the Pope's vassal, and receive and hold the Kingdom of England as from the Pope. An account of the proceedings may be seen in Baronius at the year 1172. A small portion only concerns us:—

"I, King Henry, do swear on these Holy Gospels of God that the death of Thomas, Archbishop of Canterbury, I neither planned, nor knew, nor ordered to be committed. And when I learned that that crime had been committed I was more affected with grief than if I had learned of the murder of my own son. But in this I am unable to excuse myself, that it was in consequence of excitement and anger which I had conceived against that holy man that he was killed. Wherefore, being guilty to this extent, that I appear to have given the occasion of his death, I shall. . . . Furthermore, I and my eldest son do swear that we shall receive and hold *the Kingdom of England* from our lord Pope Alexander and his Catholic successors."

Then Henry and those of the bishops who were his subjects signed this and other documents in the presence of the assembly, and these documents were subsequently solemnly proclaimed, and signed by bishops and leading men in other parts of his dominions.

Observe, first, that there is no doubt about those proceedings; they occurred in broad daylight, and occupy an undisputed place in history. Observe, secondly, that Henry was not treated as having any power over Ireland. Observe, thirdly, that the result is what is called an acquittal. Henry hardly felt it so to be thus trampled upon in the dust before the world, deprived for ever of that mastery over the Church which he had spent his life in grasping, reduced to accept his kingdom and his freedom at the hands of the Church, and only so much freedom and on such terms as she dictated. No man knew better than he that a national Church would not, and could not, have dared to treat him so. The hardfought struggle was over, the stiff neck was broken, the Church was unquestionably triumphant, and the world was called upon to witness. Acquittal, indeed! Men may call it what they please: they cannot alter its meaning. They call it an acquittal in order to induce us to believe that *one month later* Alexander wrote these letters to Henry conferring upon him more than had been involved in that long struggle, more than Henry had claimed or dreamt of claiming, more than had ever been conferred upon legate, saint, or prelate, and addressed him as one inspired by God for the conversion of the Irish, as one who had already partially converted them. What nonsense! The credulity that could believe this of Alexander would be truly colossal.

Most of what has been said applies to the remaining three letters as well as to the first. It only remains to examine their peculiarities. Cardinal Moran, while admitting the great difficulty of the question, thought these three were genuine: because they are dated at Tusculum, where the Pope was in September, 1172; because they are addressed to specified persons; and because they are inconsistent with the preceding letters. These reasons do not profess to be conclusive. The first and second attest superior skill derived from practice; the third attests inferiority in another respect, and is in the circumstances an extraordinary reason. These three ignore the preceding letters, and differ from them in substance, motive and scheme. They affect to rest upon the conquest of Ireland as an accomplished fact, and yet betray anxiety lest anything should imperil it. They make the idea of subduing and civilizing the abominable Irish originate not in Constantine's donation, nor yet in Donough O'Brien's, nor in the *Laudabiliter*, but in a Divine inspiration of Henry's—in one of Giraldus's visions, in fact. For carrying out that idea they trust not to the immemorial weapons of the Catholic Church, but to the power of Henry's united naval and military forces, with the blessing of God thrown in as an afterthought to save appearance. The letter preserved by Giraldus harmonizes with the postscript to the *Metalogicus*, but not with the *Laudabiliter*. These three harmonize with no document but themselves. But they agree perfectly with Henry's wishes. His interest is, indeed, their chief concern, the conversion of the Irish being insisted upon mainly as a means of promoting and securing his interest. That addressed to the bishops is a strong political rally on Henry's behalf. It directs the clergy to "diligently and manfully assist in subduing and retaining that land for that renowned king." It directs the bishops to censure and excommunicate whosoever should dare to resist Henry, and to "guard firmly those things which relate to the regal dignity, and, so far as in you lies, cause others to guard them;" in short, to act as policemen for Henry. There is not in the largest edition of the *Bullarium* a letter of this character from any Pope to anybody. But this letter never reached the bishops, none of these letters did, nor any letter like them.

nor any inquiry about them. The Pope never made the
English Government his channel of communication with
the Irish bishops, and except these no Papal letters have
ever been found in an English Government office addressed
to anyone in Ireland. Nor have Papal originals of these
letters ever been found. No one has ever seen a trace
of them in Rome. Baronius neither includes nor mentions
them. Not having been discovered until the eighteenth
century, they are not mentioned by any author, English
or Irish, before that time. Migne has copied them from
an English work. His reference is to Rymer's *Foedera*,
but they are not there. He must have copied them from
the *Liber Niger Scaccarii*, a work compiled from documents
kept in the English Exchequer. They are there; no one
knows who put them there, when, or on what authority;
and there is no account of the originals. It seems to me
that they never had Papal originals, and that the office
in which they were found is pretty nearly that in which
they were made. Giraldus does not appear to have been
aware of their existence, and this seems to show that he
was not deeply in the plot. Contrariwise, they differ so
essentially from the documents he preserves that they
must have been written by a different hand, which might
have been his. His authorship would be a good reason
for his silence, and would account for their extraordinary
nature. Like his sermon in Dublin, they overshot the
mark. Armed with genuine Bulls like these, Henry's
representatives in Ireland would have carried all before
them. But they should have the originals to show; copies
would be incredible. Consequently, *there was not a word
breathed about them in Ireland*. Some hundreds of years
after date what are called copies are found, *nullius
liberi*, in an English Government office. Had there been
Papal originals, would they not have lasted as long? Of
course, the so-called copies are the originals, and are of
home manufacture.

The ostensible justification of all these Bulls being alleged Irish vices, we must examine that unsavory subject in connection with the three letters in which it is expressed in the grossest manner. Lanfranc and St. Anselm, Archbishops of Canterbury, wrote some letters to Popes and to other persons, imputing barbarity and immorality to the Irish people. Neither of them had ever been in Ireland. They derived their information about it from the Danes of Dublin, Waterford and Limerick, who, wishing to be regarded as distinct from the Irish people, placed themselves under the spiritual jurisdiction of the See of Canterbury, giving a bad name to the Irish as a reason for their so doing. Canterbury, desirous of extending its jurisdiction, welcomed both the new spiritual subjects and their reasons for coming. Reasons of this character never lose in repetition. Herein we have a complete explanation of the charges contained in the letters emanating from Canterbury. That it is complete is proved by the fact that Canterbury made no attempt to improve the Irish. Jurisdiction was what Canterbury wanted. Granting that the Irish were as far from perfection as were their accusers, their faults were magnified, their virtues ignored; and the primitive condition in which the Church still remained in Ireland was itself termed a glaring vice. In constitution, discipline, and means of subsistence, the Church had too long striven to maintain its existence on the basis of the old Celtic clan upon which it had been first founded. That basis, upon which it had seen its best and holiest days, was now in a state of dissolution. The lapse of centuries, and the many changes they brought, had made some old arrangements unsuitable and new ones highly desirable, and the failure to provide these resulted in some instances in a most objectionable state of things. To men trained in the most highly developed Church of the Continent in the twelfth century, the Celtic Church, at its best, would have seemed barbarous. It was now at its very worst. The Irish themselves were quite conscious of this fact, and their consciousness was the surest guarantee that a reform was at hand. However grave the defects were, or may have appeared to high churchmen, they were vices only in a technical sense, and had never been made the ground of treating any nation as outside the pale of Christianity. Other countries remote from Rome were in a similarly backward condition, some of them to a later date. In England changes in some respects similiar to those desirable in Ireland had been effected about a century earlier. In Ireland nearly all the changes involved had been decided upon at the Synod of Kells in 1152. They were in progress when the invaders came, and it is probable that the payment of tithes was the only one of them that had not been carried into effect. The decrees of Cashel are substantially a confirmation of the decrees of Kells. The conformity aimed at was conformity with the Catholic Church, and with the English and other Churches in so far as they agreed with that standard. It is only English egotism to describe this as bringing the Irish Church into conformity with the Anglican.

St. Bernard also speaks disparagingly of the Irish. He did not know them. He speaks more severely of some people whom he did know. Doubtless, some of the "Canterbury tales" had reached him. In addition to these, Irish bishops and monks, as exacting as himself, constituted him their ghostly father, visited him on their way to and from Rome, and sought his advice on the extirpation of such vices as their flocks were addicted to. Ah! they were addicted to vices, then? Yes, and there has never been, and is not to-day, a nation free from vices; and if there is a nation that claims to be free from vices, it thereby proves that it has one vice more than other nations have. There has never been a nation either wholly pure or wholly base; and it is common knowledge that, of the highest authorities on this subject in this our age, some say that Europe is just now at its lowest state of deterioration, while others as stoutly hold that we are on the pinnacle of perfection. If we find it difficult to decide between these authoritative pronouncements on the age in which we have the privilege of living, and if, on reading the statement of one side, we are swayed to it, whether correct or not, people seven hundred years hence, if they should happen to care about us, will be greatly puzzled to know whether they ought to be proud or ashamed of us. Men like St. Bernard have a simple method of solving this difficulty. For them the world is always corrupt. Irish bishops and monks whispered their troubles into St. Bernard's ear. To do so was the chief purpose for which they visited him. Vices and irregularities necessarily formed the staple of their conversation. It was inevitable that the conviction should grow upon a man so circumstanced, who had never seen the Irish people, that vice was the only thing they were remarkable for, and that there was nothing else in Ireland worth talking about. Ah! it will be said, he was too well versed in human nature to fall into that error. Was he, though? His own nature was human, very human, as a reader of his splendid sermons will soon discover. He spoke and wrote with such fire and passion that to the present day his words almost scorch the reader's lips. He so detested vices, and the sense of their enormity so grew upon him, that, if his sweeping denunciations were to be taken literally, whether applied to Italians or to Irish, much injustice would be done. He knew not how to temporise or mince his words. Just imagine Henry II. applying to him for a certificate of character! He was a man carried away very much by the feelings of the moment, and the consequence is that, while his writings are eloquent and edifying, they are not, and were not intended to be, historically correct. Anyone of a contrary opinion cannot have read them. Where he speaks disparagingly of the

Irish is in his memoir of St. Malachy [=Mael-Maedhog O'Morgair], whom he had known and loved, and who died in his arms at Clairvaux. The effect of his eulogy of his dear friend Malachy is heightened, and intentionally and properly heightened, by painting in the blackest colours the vices and irregularities against which Malachy had contended, and over which he had triumphed. The more numerous and glaring the vices were represented to be, the greater would be Malachy's merit in having overcome them. Every vice and every irregularity mentioned by St. Bernard did exist in Ireland, and did also exist in other countries, as he well knew; but, in all probability, they existed as enormities and scandals, and not as settled manners generally prevalent. Had they been settled and general, their extirpation would have taken a much longer time to accomplish than Malachy devoted to that task. St. Bernard says:—" Accordingly, Malachy, having within three years reduced the proud, restored liberty to the Church, banished barbarity, and reformed the practice of the Christian religion everywhere, seeing all things in peace, began to think of his own peace." This is admirable; but common-sense tells us that barbarities which could be completely banished in three years could not have been very general or deeply rooted. And, as regards the barbarities themselves, we know that Continental writers used the word " barbarous " partly in the sense of "foreign," or as marking a deviation from the Continental model. One of the barbarities mentioned is the eating of porridge. Well, if St. Bernard were to return now, he would find porridge quite a fashionable dish, and might even be tempted to taste it himself. In one of his sermons he speaks of Malachy as " that burning and shining light, not yet extinct, but only removed "; one " of whom the world was not worthy "; a man whose works were " great, and many, and very good, and even better than good, because of the original intention. What work of piety escaped Malachy? He was poor towards himself, but rich towards the poor. He made himself a father to orphans, a protector to widows, a patron to the oppressed." St. Bernard's standard of perfection was the very highest. Malachy had reached it, and was the holiest and most perfect man he had ever seen. In his admiration of Malachy he did not stop to reflect that the nation which had produced that man, and many like him, could scarcely have been barbarous. His ardent nature led him rather to deal heavy blows upon all who had opposed, or thwarted, or resisted his dear friend. He was painting the character of one who had been at once very perfect and his own personal friend. The opponents and the vices that friend had actually overcome were an essential part of the picture, and the darker they were made, the brighter Malachy shone. St. Bernard's picture on the whole is really a bright one by force of Malachy's character alone. He knew well that Malachy's sanctity was not singular in Ireland, and that by including other Irishmen he might with equal truth have made his picture much brighter. He was not dealing with others. His subject was Malachy and whatsoever had crossed Malachy's path. This explains the whole position and goes far to neutralize sweeping charges. The statement that Malachy had succeeded in making all things right in the short space of three years completes the correction from St. Bernard's own mouth.

The greatest abuse with which Malachy had to deal was of a local and personal nature. It was the pretended inheritance of Church property by laymen who, taking advantage of disorders occasioned by Danish irruptions and accidental favouring circumstances of corruption, weakness and apathy, had in a few places assumed the titles and all the worldly goods of bishops and abbots, leaving the ecclesiastics who strove to discharge the duties of those offices stripped of their means of living. In this way a certain family had seized upon all the property belonging to the primatial See of Armagh and held it in spite of all complaints for many generations, until at last Malachy succeeded in dislodging them at the risk of his life. This abuse was no part of the Celtic ecclesiastical system, but was a symptom of the decay of that system; and it was the cause of troubles and scandals in various parts of Europe as well as in Ireland. And the action of Henry II. in keeping Sees vacant and appropriating their revenues, which the Pope frequently condemned, differed from the abuse at Armagh only in being the action of a king, while that at Armagh was the action of a private family.

The other foul vices attributed to the Irish people by some of the eminent men named, and more grossly and offensively by Giraldus and by one of the letters we are now considering, demand little notice from us even if their nature permitted of their discussion in clean pages. All that has been said on exaggeration applies to them more forcibly than to the abuses with which we have dealt. It is part of fallen human nature to exaggerate such things. Vague slanders without names to connect them with could not have been verified when written, and still less can they be verified now. They are intangible things, shadows without substance. They may or may not have been transmitted in huge quantities by Englishmen to the Pope. If Englishmen say they were, we are not called upon to dispute. But that would not make them true. They would remain slanders and nothing more. The Pope would not have acted without inquiring. If he believed the slanders, his condemnation if strong would have been, as on all occasions, decent. He knew it would not lose but gain in strength by being decent. His language was always decent even when dealing with matters as bad as these letters represent. On no other occasion did he use language unfit to be translated. It is an outrage no less upon his memory than upon the Irish people to say that he wrote the second of these letters to Henry. Had he been greatly moved by a false report, and written a strong condemnation, he would have seen that it reached the Bishops and that they acted upon it. He never inquired about these letters. His subsequent action was that of a man who had no knowledge of them ; and that was in fact his position. In all his genuine letters—and there are 1,520 of them in Migne's collection—there is not one expression of an indecent character. Of that great number the only letters that are unworthy of him are—the letter ordering the imprisonment of Thomas à Becket as an idiot, and these letters treating the Irish as horrible savages. All these were written in Henry's interest. Migne brands the first as a forgery. We brand the others as forgeries. The vices like the letters were of English manufacture. The inclusion of them in the letters proves that. Beyond spurning them we have little to say to them. Slanders different but as bad have been levelled against ourselves in the nineteenth century, and supported by forgeries too. We reject them all, the ancient and the modern. Our ancestors were a healthy people who enjoyed pure air and country life. Like ourselves, they were probably far from being perfect. Let their accusers apply that simple test to themselves and confess the result. There are few pages of the Irish annals of the twelfth century that do not record the death of some good man or woman distinguished for charity, piety, learning and wisdom. These people had spent all their lives in Ireland. Are we to be told that all the good people were dead or dying, and that criminals alone were healthy? It would seem so. What then of the good people? What were they good for, if they left none but criminals behind them? Their good name was not merely local nor ill-founded. Three Irishmen of that century are enrolled among the Saints of the Universal Church, and much other Irish merit can be equally well verified. Vague slanders are evasive and can never be verified. The state in which an Irishman could believe them would be a state of disease. To set him right he would need not argument but air and exercise. A sickly student of Darwinism once threw up his hands in despair exclaiming that it was folly to expect that men could ever become noble or even respectable since they were all descended from monkeys. His doctor recommended the excitement of the chase. His friends, with much difficulty, induced him to follow the advice. After a few months the youth, restored to health, laughed heartily at Darwinism and the monkeys.

The Pope is represented as saying that he had received a succession of letters from the Irish bishops to the effect that Henry had already partially succeeded in converting the Irish, a work in which presumably the bishops had spent all their lives in vain. What a probable statement that is. Through Henry's power, crimes had begun to diminish, and the seeds of virtue to sprout in place of vice. A learned supporter of these ridiculous letters says that the vices of the Irish were not due to the invasion, as is commonly supposed, but were old and permanent, because they were such as could not have sprung up in the short space of a few years; but he finds no difficulty in accepting as genuine a letter according to which Henry had already succeeded in bringing back the Irish to some degree of virtue, although he had spent only six months in the country and had visited only a small portion of it. Had Henry spent six months more in the country the Irish would have become too holy for anything. It was lucky that he had to hurry off to kiss the dust at Avranches. His prompt success as a lay missionary over the inveterate vices of a whole nation which bishops and clergy had long contended against in vain, may be left to the judgment of real missionaries who usually find their task more difficult. If it were true, they should revise

their methods. Pope Alexander would need to be
extremely credulous to belive such a story, and to believe
it too of the very man who had given him the most trouble.
The Irish annalists did not believe it. Giraldus did not
believe it, but confessed on his death-bed that the effect
of the invasion was to make the condition of everything
worse. The Irish bishops did not believe it and did not
write it, because they had personal knowledge of the fact
that the country was just then more distracted than it
had been at any previous period of its history. The
English clergymen present at the Synod of Cashel, having
come expecting a barbarous country, and finding it
civilized and provided with a hierarchy and clergy and
ample means for its own regeneration, reported to that
effect to the King, and in doing so probably gave him
some credit for what they considered a change, but what
was no change except in the amount of their knowledge.
This report supplied the idea of Henry's missionary
success.

The same gentleman, whom I regret having had to
allude to so often, tells us that considerations of decency
prevented Alexander from saying anything in the last
of these letters to Henry in reference to the *denarius* or
penny reserved by the *Laudabiliter* for the Roman See.
If the supposed decent silence was expected to help in
proving the authenticity of these letters, will those who
use it for that purpose allow that the indecent expression
of that same matter in the letter in question is of equal
force in proving its falseness? and if not, why not? On
turning back to this letter it will be seen that a whole
paragraph of it is devoted to the reservation of the Peter's
pence.

A *denarius*—the word usually translated "penny"—
had a purchasing power equal to about 4s. 10d. of our
money. Hence a *denarius* from every house in Ireland
would have amounted to a considerable sum. The invaders

were in no hurry to pay it for themselves: nor did they transmit to the Pope any *denarii* they succeeded in taking from the Irish. The careful reservation of the *denarius* in these letters may have been intended to serve the double purpose of aiming a sly joke at the Pope, as Giraldus once did, and of giving an additional air of probability to the letters by suggesting the motive of lucre.

It has been urged with much energy that if those letters were spurious Pope Alexander's successor would have denounced them on their first appearance. Would he? He never denounced the Bull condemning St. Thomas à Becket to prison for life, and yet it is spurious. Like case like rule.

To prove a negative is proverbially difficult, and by some held to be impossible. It is sometimes possible when the negative is true. But to prove it is not sufficient; and what remains to be done is still more difficult—to fix the proof in the memory. The function of the memory is to retain positive facts, whether true or false. Positive facts, whether true or false, are the only real facts, and are the proper objects of the memory. False statements that are positive, and things that are spurious, share the advantage of true facts in being easily retained in the memory, partly because they have the appearance of truth, and partly, also, because, although false, they are in a limited sense positive facts. A spurious bank-note is a tangible thing, which may be taken in the hand and read, and the making, circulation, and effect of which, being positive facts, the memory will retain as easily as if the note were genuine. If the maker has negotiated the note, will you expect him to admit that it was made by him? Of course not. He will stoutly maintain that it was made by the bank, and not by him. He will point to the value he has received for it as proof of its genuineness. If it has circulated through the hands of other persons, he will point to every one of them as witnesses that they believed it and exchanged it for value or value for it, and, therefore, that it is true. Persons who have seen it in business or casually, conform their words and acts to it as genuine, and thus, quite unconscious of wrong, facilitate its circulation and give it increased vigour and vitality. At first having no inherent force, and being sickly, it is negotiated with caution, and apart from other notes: but with every new believer, however acquired, it gathers plausibility and strength until at length it becomes like unto true notes, and more aggressive than they. Every incident in its career is a positive fact, which takes a position in the memory as readily, and holds it as tenaciously, as if the note were genuine. To make and start the false instrument was somebody's interest. To maintain it may be the interest of several. All who recognise it in any way help to maintain it. To refute it may be the interest of a number so large that it may not be the special business of any person in particular. If there should be a person so curious, what he has to prove is that the note was *not* made by the bank. That is a negative fact—that is to say, although true, it is not a fact at all, but the absence of a fact. He has to dislodge a real, though false, fact, which already holds position in the memory, and to give the memory instead no object to lay hold of and retain. He has to create a mental vacuum where before there was something actual, no matter what. This is no easy feat. He may succeed in accomplishing it; but what remains to be done is more difficult still, if not impossible. He has to ask people to keep clearly before their minds not a fact, but the absence of a dislodged fact. This is work for which the memory is not adapted, and few people even try to force it into service.

To prove that the letters before us were not written by the Popes to whom they are attributed would be an undertaking precisely analogous. It would be to prove a negative; and as hardly anyone would remember that proof, however true, the result would be *nil*. At first the impure substance was there; we have burned it away, and soon the process is forgotten. Herein lies the inherent weakness of negative evidence, and, therefore, the weakest element and greatest practical defect in the case against these letters. Prove as we may, the mere mention of them by anybody is flourished as a positive fact, while the number of historical works, Irish, English, and Continental, in which they ought to appear and do not, is, though enormous, wholly ignored because it is negative. Each such case of non-appearance is a fact, important, relevant, and before reason, of equal weight with each appearance. The number of cases in which the letters should, if genuine, appear, and do not appear, is so great, that if reason were our sole guide the few cases in which they do appear would be beneath notice. But the few, being positive facts, are remembered, while the many are not so much forgotten as not noticed. Even if we follow these letters to the few works in which they are included, their condition is little better. Of the five letters, one edition of the *Bullarium* contains only one; four are absent. Another edition contains only one; four are absent. Another edition contains two; three are absent. Another edition contains not one of the five; five are absent. Here, if the letters were genuine, we should have twenty appearances. There are only four. These four are trumpeted and remembered. The sixteen non-appearances, though logically of four times the weight, are ignored because they are negative facts, that is the absence of positive facts. This inherent element of weakness affects not alone this one argument based upon numbers, but every argument against these letters. It is this all-pervading defect in the case against them that has kept them from being crushed out of existence long ago. Like flies on the wound of a chained animal, their life depends not on their own strength, but on our physical limitations.

Appearance or non-appearance in a *Bullarium* does not prove anything. It is only evidence. The *Bullarium* is not an official collection, but the work of a private compiler, and, as a body, has no authority, but stands precisely on the same level with any other large collection of ancient writings. So far as the documents are genuine, each carries its own authority derived from its source. If the collection is large the compiler does not undertake that all the documents it contains are authentic, still less does he profess to make them so. He may be in doubt about some, and he may consider an ancient document of sufficient historical interest to be worth preserving, even if he knows that it is spurious. In the case of most Papal letters Continental compilers had before them either the original documents bearing their appropriate seals and regularly authenticated, or verified copies derived from proper custody; and no question of authenticity arising, the documents were included as a matter of course. In the case of documents like these relating to Ireland, which are neither originals nor verified copies, which come from no one knows what source, of which all that can be said is that they are produced by parties interested, a Continental compiler taking no special interest in them, having no means of testing and no incentive to test them, simply includes or rejects them at his good pleasure, or according to the exigencies of space, or for some reason irrespective of their value or want of value. In the ultimate result the editor who included the *Laudabiliter* in the *Bullarium* has, by exposing its imperfection, done more to bring discredit upon it than the editor who excluded it.

It is something that in the language of the Gael which was spoken and written in Ireland in the twelfth century, and for many centuries after, there is not a word to confirm or recognise these letters. It is something that, with all our weaknesses and disadvantages, we have, without

emptying our quiver, inflicted upon the cause of the
Bulls wounds beyond number as they are beyond healing.
It is something to have, once for all, given their advocates
a task of extracting arrows which will occupy them for
the rest of their lives. It is something that we now leave
them in such a condition that to restore them would be
far more difficult than to provide new ones. For I have
no doubt what my readers' verdict will be. It has not
been snatched prematurely. It will be as correct, final,
and conclusive as a verdict on circumstantial evidence
ever can be. It will be a moral certitude as indefectible
as any merely human knowledge ever can be. It will
be founded so strongly that it can never be shaken or
disturbed by argument, by evidence, by aught less cogent
than the production of a real Bull *Laudabiliter*, bearing
its leaden seal. It will be a spontaneous growth from the
evidence, and no more the work of my head or hands than
was, say, Constantine's donation. Ah! that dear donation
which has proved for forgers and their defenders so much
dearer than they bargained for! And the dear postcript
to the *Metalogicus*, which tattered what it was intended
to support, and scattered the fragments to the winds.
And the oath of stony-hearted John of Salisbury that
forgers had used his name. Cruel John! It was pure
modesty that induced the forgers to write your name
instead of their own. Modesty hath trials. Forgers are
the most retiring people in the world. It is with the
greatest difficulty they can be found when "wanted." It
is with the greatest reluctance they come into the—dock.
Instances are known of their retiring from the dock "for
life." Modesty can no farther go. Very thoughtful and
kind to Henry these forgers were. They knew his inmost
desire and what the rest of the world ought to have done
for him but did not. They had a special knowledge of
what Popes ought to have done for him but did not.
Without obtruding their own personality upon the public

they showed the way, conferred upon Henry every power they could think of, spiritual and temporal, with a generous hand, and consigned troublesome Thomas à Becket to prison for life. There was true friendship. They had the right idea of how the world ought to be regenerated. And we must not forget Giraldus, to whom we owe, besides his numerous and opportune visions, the destruction of his own evidence. Nor can we omit an acknowledgment of our indebtedness to those clever messengers who got Bulls "at Rome," where there was no Pope at the time; and Bishop Rotrodus, who did get a real Bull, but so different from the one he wanted. It would be the basest ingratitude were we to close without paying our tribute of praise to the gentlemen who have hitherto supported these Bulls, for the trouble they have taken in discovering instances in which Popes and Cardinals have been induced to say things for which there was absolutely no foundation. And we shall always remember with pleasure the excellent arguments which those same gentlemen have adduced in support of the Bulls—excellent for toppling before a crooked look. All these are positive facts of a class for which our memory is receptive and retentive: and they amount to something in a cause which we were told was lost.

To add to them there is one thing more. Where are the Bulls? As I said at the outset, the first step in our inquiry should have been the production and proof of the documents themselves. It is a usual and strictly just requirement. It is essential, and could not fail to be of the utmost importance. It, and nothing less, could amount to positive proof. We waived it for the time, in order to allow the argument to proceed, and to test such circumstantial evidence as could be offered. This we have tested, and the test has proved fatal to it. Had it all been valid it could not have done more than increase the amount of probability. The originals would still be required.

We have found none of it valid, much of it worthless, some of it positively destructive of the Bulls. If more evidence of the same character were discovered, the first use that could be made of it is to submit it to us, that we might take it in both hands and test its value. There is no use in proceeding further without the original documents. We have heard and said enough about them, and want to see them. The originals have never been produced. No verified copies of them have ever been produced. No fac-similes of them have ever been produced, as has been done in the case of genuine Bulls of the same century. Some hundreds of volumes of State Papers and other documents illustrative of English history have been published by private persons, by historical societies, by institutions, and by the State; and not one of them contains an authoritative reproduction of any of these Bulls from the originals, nor is it stated in one of them that the originals anywhere exist, or ever existed. Of the six letters in form Papal written in the interest of King Henry II. one was designed to assist him in crushing St. Thomas of Canterbury and the other five were designed to assist him in crushing Ireland. Three of the six, though expressly urgent, were not published for some centuries after date. One of the six is branded as spurious by a Continental critic of unquestionable impartiality. It was written by Henry's servants or sycophants, and, therefore, never had a Papal original. We have found reasons more than sufficient for affixing a like brand to the other five, written equally in the interest of the same king. If they are to escape that brand, obviously it can only be by the production and proof of authentic Papal originals; and the beneficiaries under them, who claim to have been their custodians, have left themselves without a word to excuse them from that duty. They have had the documents long enough in their keeping and in their affections, and can certainly not complain when at length they are invited to prove them absolutely by letting others see the originals besides those who profit under them. The fact that no original of any one of them ever has been shown can be due only to impossibility. It cannot be attributed to want of will, nor to want of skill; and surely it is not our fault. It is not sufficient to rail at our incredulity. We are all ready to believe the documents, to believe anything, on adequate evidence. This being the only evidence that in the premisses can be adequate, as soon as it is produced, but not till then, our adhesion is assured. The original parchments of earlier and of later Bulls, bearing their appropriate seals, are still extant, and fac-similes of them may be seen in Rymer's *Fœdera* and other books accessible to the public. We now want the originals or fac-similes of these. It is admitted that if these were originally genuine they must have been cast in the form usual with the Popes to whom they are ascribed. What are produced as copies do not present that form, and are, therefore, not correct copies of true Bulls. The production of originals or fac-similes in that form is essential to any attempt to maintain their genuineness, and until it has been done there is nothing to disprove. He who affirms must prove. This is no case for casual or factitious evidence, the primary assertion being that formal evidence of the highest character was pre-constituted, and that the beneficiaries made the preservation of it the object of their special solicitude. Whoever, for any purpose, affirms that these Bulls are genuine, represents the beneficiaries to that extent, and is not entitled to be heard until he has produced the Bulls from Winchester Castle, or wherever he can find them. Since the day the statement was written that they were preserved in that castle, the purpose of holding a grip of Ireland has never been abandoned, and the care of all that strengthened that grip has never been relaxed. Very good. This, if anything, is what they were preserved for—to be produced when required. They are required now. The requirement is not a hard one, but strictly just. What is hard and terribly inconvenient is, to be unable to produce on the ultimate test, documents with which one has insulted a people, and which one has boasted of guarding. That is hard and humiliating. Originals of genuine Bulls as old still exist. What reason but spuriousness can account for the absence of these? Why were they not produced in the twelfth century when fresh and new? Why were they not produced in the twelfth, thirteenth, and fourteenth centuries, when, according to the English themselves, the Irish commonly regarded them as false, and when the production of them would have at once and for ever settled that vital question? Why but because no original Bulls corresponding to these papers ever existed? Let him who affirms the contrary prove it, as authentic instruments are proved—by producing the originals. Failing to do this, let him go and bury the false Bulls with the false donation in the stillest oblivion.

I owe an apology for the excessive care with which I have removed dust and cobwebs from documents which each fresh light showed to be base and worthless. Further examination of them would be unpardonable. The Popes never wrote them nor caused them to be written. Falsae sunt, et eis ad delusionem nostram, et sui damnationem solus falsarius scienter usus est.

END.

INDEX.

	PAGE
ADMISSION of English	118
Adrian IV.	6, 14, 102
Alciato, Cardinal	122
Alexander III.	16, 39, 131
Alexander VI.	30
Ambition of English hierarchy	105, 106, 141
Anselm, St.	13, 141
Avranches, proceedings at	137
BALTINGLASS, Abbot of	66
Baronius, Cardinal	28, 105, 137
Becket, St. Thomas à	39, 132, 133, 135, 137
Benedict, Abbot of Peterborough	12
Bernard, St.	13, 103, 142
Bishops, nomination of	107
Bruce, Edward	117
Bullarium	33, 153
Bulls never produced	155, 156
Bull, genuine	110
Bull, spurious	136
CALIXTUS III.	30
Cambrensis Eversus	56
Cambrensis, Giraldus	13, 21, 49
Cashel, Synod of	83, 113
Conclave, le	11
Constantine the Great	10, 12, 28
Cumin, John	66
DANISH colonists	13, 107, 141
De Courci, John	79
Denarius	104, 149
Diceto, Ralph De	13
Dimock, Rev. James	22, 60
FALLACY of late evidence	123
Felix, Bishop of Ossory	69
Fitz Aldelin	81, 87
Fitz Bernard	81

	PAGE
Fitz Girald	51, 77
Forgeries, to send to France for	112
Forgers, modesty of	154
Frederick Barbarossa	102
Freeman, Mr.	61
GELASIUS, Archbishop of Armagh	84
Gilbert's *History of the Viceroys*	73
Giraldus Cambrensis	13, 21, 49
Gregory VII.	11
HARRIS	100
Haverty	89
Hearne, Thomas	16, 118
Henry II.	38, 72, 73, 74, 133, 137
Henry's letter of congratulation	105
Henry VIII.	5, 120
Hereditary right	26, 39, 40
Hovenden, Roger de	13, 80
Hubert, Archbishop of Canterbury	99
Humiliation of Henry II.	137
INNOCENT X.	123
Irish morality	103, 141
JOHN XXII.	29, 115
John of Salisbury	23, 48, 105
KELLY, Rev. M.	7, 56
Kells, Synod of	104, 142
Kilkenny, Confederation of	123
LABBE	83, 87
Lanfranc	13, 141
Lanigan, Rev. Dr.	3, 114
Le Mans, Bishop of	105
Liber Niger Scaccarii	16, 140
Limitation of King's power	107
Limitation of Pope's power	124
Lingard, Dr.	131

	PAGE
Lisieux, Bishop of	105
Louis, King of France	109
Lynch, Rev. John	55, 96, 100
Macariæ Excidium	57
Mac Morrough, Dermot	77
Malachy, St.	144
Malone, Very Rev. Dr. 3, 6, 31, 58, 114, 119, 135, 148, 149	
Marianus	103
Martyrless Ireland	67, 69
Merlin Celidon	75, 79
Metalogicus	23, 26
Migne	16, 41, 87, 135, 147
Model Bull	109, 110, 112
Moran, Cardinal	3, 87, 106, 118, 138
Morris, Rev. W. B.	3, 41, 89
Murder of Becket	79, 135
NEGATIVE, to prove a	150
Nicholas V.	30
Nicholas of Wallingford	87
OATH that forgery had been committed	43
O'Brien, Donough	114
O'Callaghan, J. C.	57
O'Connor, Roderick	112
O'Kelly, Colonel Charles	57
Oneyle, Donald	116
O'Rourke, Prince of Breifny	76
O'Toole, St. Laurence	64, 90, 126
PAPARO, Cardinal	103
Paris, Matthew	13, 106
Paul IV.	119
Peter of Blois	115
Pole, Cardinal	120

	PAGE
Policraticus	43
Possibility of forgery	21, 22, 27, 28
REMONSTRANCE	115
Retractations of Giraldus	99
Richey	128
Rinuccini	123
Robert de Monte	45
Roger, Archbishop of York	133
Rotrodus, Bishop	105, 109, 112
SALISBURY, John of	23, 48, 105
Scotichronicon	118
Sixtus IV.	30
Specialist, the Pope not a	124
St. Albans, Abbot of	36, 105, 109
Sylvester	12, 28
Synods	80, 83
THOMAS, St.	39, 132, 133, 135, 136, 137
Tithes	12, 142
URBAN II.	11, 29
Ussher, James	3, 126
VISIONS	75, 79
Vivianus, Cardinal	73, 88
WARE, Sir James	68, 95
Wendover, Roger de	13, 106
Where are the Bulls ?	155
White, Rev. Stephen, S.J.	3, 55, 74
Wilkins	87, 88
Winchester	31, 87
Wonders of Ireland	91
YORK, Archbishop of	133
ZINKEISEN, Dr.	126

www.ingramcontent.com/pod-product-compliance
Lightning Source LLC
Chambersburg PA
CBHW030252170426
43202CB00009B/718